MAN, GOD, AND THE MAN-GODS OF ANTIQUITY

ADAMOS ZAGARA

Archway Publishing books may be ordered through booksellers or by contacting:

Archway Publishing
1663 Liberty Drive
Bloomington, IN 47403
www.archwaypublishing.com
844-669-3957

ISBN: 978-1-6657-4694-6 (sc)
ISBN: 978-1-6657-4695-3 (e)

Library of Congress Control Number: 2023913041

Print information available on the last page.

Archway Publishing rev. date: 07/17/2023

INTRODUCTION

Anthropological and archaeological evidence has revealed that upright walking hominids have been around for millions of years and lived almost all of that time as stone-age hunter-gatherers that evolved rather slowly throughout our maturation into the human of today. It is likely that many variations of hominids evolved and, later, died out as a result of natural selection, the pressures of ever-changing environmental conditions, and perhaps even a worldwide catastrophe or two. At about seven to twelve thousand years ago, sudden, profound changes occurred with regards to mankind. We became very intelligent and began organizing ourselves into city-states and other relatively large urban communities. Towns were planned and built complete with fresh water sources, sewage systems, and centralized leadership. Archaeological evidence indicates that this appears to have happened almost overnight, as compared to the amount of time we spent as Stone Age hunter-gatherers. How was this suddenly possible, and what was the trigger? Did God intervene on behalf of humanity? Is there another rational explanation that does not include aliens? Finally, what does our recorded history tell us about these dramatic changes in our behavior? Is any of this history relavent to us now— and in the future?

The Modern Theory of Evolution

Together, we will examine some of the most important sources of information about our past as well as some of the more recent archaeological discoveries that are proving our past is not at all what we have been taught. We will examine exactly what it means to be human. We will also strive to understand why humans have such a need to be controlled by a greater power or God. Somewhere between humanity and God, our past is full of stories of what I call the man-gods of antiquity. In my opinion, not enough attention has been given to these mighty heroes of old, aside from brief references to myths and legends that are found in various cultures around the world. What if these creatures of legend were actually offspring of the gods living on Earth side by side with our ancient relatives? Maybe it is nothing more than fantasy and nonsense. Besides, who in their right mind would believe in such a story?

Modern Religious Scripture (Western)

CHAPTER

In the Beginning

It is in our nature as humans to question our realities as we grow and experience the world around us. We recognize ourselves and other humans as being separate and distinct from all other animal species on our little planet. What is it, exactly, that makes humans so much more intelligent and likely to remain at the top of the food chain? More important, how did we get this way? The narrative that most of us are familiar with is based on ancient writings that have been passed down from antiquity and now form the backbone of religious texts around the world. Although every culture seems to have a different take on the details, there are a surprising number of similarities that are shared. One particularly interesting common thread is the story of the gods creating humanity in their image. Another is the story of the sons of the gods and how they fell out of favor with the older gods. Also, we cannot forget the creation story and the flood story. In the flood story, the gods wanted to destroy humankind and start over with a clean slate because of the dirty deeds of the fallen ones, who took human women for wives and created abominable offspring. Yeah, that story really is written in the Old Testament.

The oldest and most important scriptures for all the people of the Christian, Jewish, and Islamic faiths come from the same source. Modern scriptures are based on the Old Testament, the New Testament—which is not accepted by the Jewish faith— and other scriptures of relevance as decided by humans who are more knowledgeable than God. Collectively referred to as "books," the compiled selection of ancient scriptures is called the Bible, and most people do not even know what it is or how it came to be. The word "*bible*", as used today, comes from the Greek word "*biblion*", meaning something akin to "paper scroll" or "papyrus scroll". However, it is likely that "*biblion*" has its roots from Byblos, a Phoenician port from which papyrus from Egypt was exported to Greece. Perhaps, in antiquity, the writings were referred to as *Scriptio Biblios* (Latin) and later, when anglicized, shortened to "the Bible."

Many people cannot tell the differences between the Old Testament and the New Testament. They were told to call it the Bible, so that is what they call it. They were also told that it contained the very words of God. Bear with me on this subject matter, because it is important to understand where some of our history comes from. As I understand it, the Christian Bible as we know it did not even exist prior to the establishment of a collection of scripts that were deemed suitable for inclusion into the canon of scripture by early church figures sometime in the first millennium CE. There is a long-but-interesting story about how the Bible was compiled into what is referred to as "books" by most scholars, and it is really something that should be explained clearly in our education system. With regard to the Hebrew Bible, which predates the Christian version, I have never even heard of any Jewish discoveries that would suggest that the teachings of the Torah were being observed by the Jewish people in general until sometime during the first millennium BCE. I am aware that the rituals and laws of the Jewish faith were being taught at that time, but it seems that worship and practices outside of the Torah's teachings were also popular among the people of that age.

I am not a biblical scholar by any means, but for me, the most telling part of the story of the Bible concerns the "books" that were excluded from the Bible— and it wasn't God who excluded them. So, the Christians have their Bible with the Old and New Testaments, and Islam has the Koran, and the Jews have the Torah, which is comprised of the first five books of the Old Testament— the same first five books you will find in any Christian Bible. The Jewish Bible came first, with the Torah and other scriptures collectively called the Tanakh, followed by the Christian Bible, with a gradual formality being realized sometime around the second or third century CE. Finally, Islam came along in the seventh century CE. The Old Testament scriptures, as recorded in the Torah, have changed the least over the ages, but many scholars debate some of the translations, so we are still left to make up our own minds about what is truth and what is fiction. Also, we may never know which or how many ancient writings were never included in the first place simply because they had been discarded or lost to time. The reason I take the time to discuss all of this is because, to understand the differences between humanity, God, and the man-gods, we must research any and all of the information available to come to a logical conclusion that, at least, leans toward the truth of the matter. So many questions! Do we take literally what is written in the books of the Bible, or can we be satisfied with what some religious authoritarian tells us it means? Are scriptures the words of God, or are they just the words of many people over a vast period of time— so long, in fact, that they have become holy simply by the nature of their antiquity? After all, you can't question the long-dead authors of those documents. Could it be that we are still being brainwashed in order for others to maintain their hold on us? Can we believe anything we read in modern scripture, or is it all just bedtime stories? To truly understand this subject matter, we must start at the beginning— if we can find it!

It is impossible to say with any certainty exactly when humans developed religious behaviors. As far as that goes, when did we become human in the first place? Perhaps we need to look at these questions more critically than in the past. Most scholars would agree that we did not become bipedal overnight. It is also likely that our evolutionary path to the physical hominids we are today is quite convoluted and is the result of a mixture of various primate species. The next time you see a chimpanzee on television or at the zoo, take a minute or two to look very closely at him or her. Humans and chimps share almost 99 percent of the same DNA. A 2005 genome study that compared chimp and human DNA revealed a difference of only about 1.23 percent. For me, that is extraordinary news! Do you think we humans really have the right to classify ourselves into races after learning that? All of the human population on planet Earth is of one family, no matter what our physical appearances say and no matter what any bigot tells you!

We Are All One Big Family

If we are to believe the history we have been taught, it is just a case of evolving slowly over time and learning by observation and repetition, adapting to changing environments, and maybe just a little luck as well. Truth is that environmental pressures play a large role in how we evolve, but again, these changes usually occur over many generations and occur in almost immeasurable amounts of change per iteration. It is therefore safe to say that moving out of the trees to roaming the Savannah as upright, bipedal creatures probably took place over the course of a few hundred to several thousands of years. It is also likely that this transformation occurred in various parts of the world in overlapping and maybe even simultaneous patterns. This is just my opinion, but I think it explains in part why there were so many variations in protohuman populations. Just being bipedal, however, does not automatically make one a human. Our history lessons also speak of some sort of interventions that, from time to time, caused changes in our mental and physical abilities. There are various theories about how these changes may have produced advantageous traits or conditions that resulted in accelerated increases in the population growth of our ancestors. One must consider that it is only the past several thousand years that humanity has grown in great numbers and has spread out to occupy much, if not most, of the landmass on the planet. Please remember that this is the modern textbook theory, which is in serious need of an update.

As recently as about six thousand years ago, humans lived mostly in areas relatively close to sources of water, such as rivers, lakes, and, of course, oceans and seas. Generally speaking, where there is water, there is food. Living near salty bodies of water may have made for easy fishing, but it also meant that you had to find freshwater from streams or natural wells, which are not available everywhere. Much of the inland areas remained basically unsettled and sparsely populated. Where freshwater was available, communities grew until the environment could no longer support the size of the population. Societies were mostly congregated along rivers, and large population centers were few and far between— or so we were taught. The lessons in our history books are just one take on the development of humans. There are also other theories that, at first glance, seem to be too far-fetched to be taken seriously. In recent years, however, the Earth has effectively become a smaller planet. With the advent of modern technology, especially social media, we are much more closely connected to one another, and information is just a mouse-click away. For the most part, what one person knows, anyone can know. From print and broadcast media to reputable online sources of information, such as universities and independent research facilities, knowledge is available to almost anyone interested in learning.

So, when did it all begin for humankind? Almost everyone has heard the phrase "In the beginning …" or some similar words that relate to a creation story. Every culture on the planet seems to have its own creation myth explaining how the universe and humans came into being. What I find intriguing is that many disparate cultures seem to have similar stories. It is as if every culture can trace its particular legend back to a common source in some far, distant time. Eons before stories were recorded in written form, storytelling was the main method of transferring knowledge and history down through the generations. This could have been accomplished in many different ways, such as through recitals on special occasions, recitals during regular ceremonial or religious events, and even through songs and poems.

How far back into antiquity can we go and say with any certainty that some culture was practicing an oral tradition? We do know that as far back as approximately 5500 BCE, pictorial writing was in use in Mesopotamia in the vicinity of modern Iraq. One can infer that storytelling was in vogue for hundreds or even thousands of years before that. Humans did not learn to speak and communicate with one another overnight. Several languages are credited with being in use around 6000 BCE, such as Hebrew, Tamil, and Egyptian. Putting together just a couple pieces of the puzzle points to stories being handed down for maybe thousands of years prior. Wait— that's a giant leap! Remember that many cultures around the world have very similar features in their creation myths and stories of the gods and their powers.

One story that stands out above the rest is the story of a great flood. Yes, likely the one that is referred to in the texts of modern religions. For cultures everywhere around the world to have a collective memory of such an event, it must have been caused by a catastrophe occurring on a global scale in a far, distant past. Modern science has revealed that there actually have been several catastrophes because of environmental changes that occurred globally. One such event is likely to have occurred as recently as 12,500 years ago, which, according to modern theories, caused so much fresh water to flow into the oceans that many coastal areas flooded and temperatures suddenly warmed after a frigid period of over a thousand years.

The illustration below is for reference only and is not meant to be precise. Note the great variability in climate that was occurring around the time humanity was becoming established as the dominant species on our planet. The most notable fact is not how much temperature variability our ancestors dealt with, but, more important, the speed at which the temperature was able to rebound from extremely frigid conditions to temperatures closer to what we experience today. Global warming is nothing new, and as far as we know, people had nothing to do with it many thousands of years ago. We may, however, be looking at another dive into our icy past that will occur in our near future. Nature's cycles repeat and repeat and repeat.

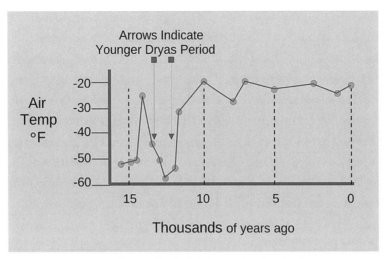

Arrows Indicate
Younger Dryas Period

Air
Temp
°F

Younger Dryas Period: Illustration by Author

Note that in the Greenland temperature graph above, there was a sudden temperature spike approximately 14,700 years ago. This was followed by a period of steady cooling for hundreds of years where the temperature bottomed out at nearly sixty below (Fahrenheit) during the period referred to by geologists as the Younger Dryas period. Then suddenly, about 12,500 years ago, we see the same thing happen that occurred back around 14,700 years ago. It was another very sudden huge spike in temperature. These events were global warming on steroids. Both environmental disasters are equally likely to have caused relatively sudden and dramatic rises in sea levels. If another ice age began today, I am sure that few humans would remain a thousand years from now, and they would be living as hunter-gatherers. Please also note that, for the last ten thousand years, temperatures have been much warmer, thus providing a more suitable environment for hominids to thrive. In fact, we are presently living in an interglacial period in Earth's climate history. It is no surprise to me that a real flood story exists to this day, even if there were no written records that far back in time. Well, maybe there were and we just haven't found them yet. History is not static, and there are no guarantees that another ice age won't occur— maybe sooner than you think!

Although there is still much debate over the causes and effects related to these climatic changes, there is no question that it was an actual occurrence that left its fingerprint clearly visible on the planet and in the minds of humans. Various scientists, including archaeologists, geologists, and meteorologists, are all in agreement about the reality of these events. Actually, it seems as if we are experiencing the beginning of a climate disruption now as we end the first quarter of the twenty-first century. We are presently experiencing what appears to be climate warming. Huge quantities of ice are shedding fresh water into the oceans, diluting the salt concentration of the water. This disrupts the current conveyors in the world's oceans, and that has a direct effect on climate, both regional and global. Events such as these are constantly changing the landscape, turning tundra into farmland and savannahs into deserts. The current warming trend we are experiencing can be stopped or even reversed quite quickly with the advent of a sudden period of large-scale volcanism. Similar events are recorded all throughout the geological record. In fact, as of February 2023, at least twenty-two volcanoes were reported as active, as per the Smithsonian Institute's Global Volcanism Program. As I sit here quietly typing this story, there are twenty-six volcanoes erupting lava and gases in various locations around the globe, many in populated areas.

Ash Cloud Eruption

Many large mammals died out during the Younger Dryas period, and likely much of the hominid population as well. It is possible that there were quite a few varieties of hominids walking the planet prior to the Younger Dryas period. It must have been an extremely stressful time for hominids, including humans, and that stress may have triggered genetic changes that actually helped us to survive as a species. Recent archaeological discoveries have revealed that at least three species of humans were sharing the planet at that time. More on that later, but here's the point: If the global flood event at the end of the

Younger Dryas was the flood of the Bible, the Koran, the Torah, and other religious texts and cultural myths, then it is obvious that oral tradition was being utilized almost thirteen thousand years ago. That must be how the knowledge of these events was passed down through the generations until they were written in stone sometime around 5000 BCE.

I believe this answers the question about how far back in time we can possibly trace oral tradition with any certainty. Fifty years from now, however, people might laugh about how ignorant we were in 2023 as more artifacts are discovered around the world. At some point, we might learn that civilization is much, much older. The flood story is not the only story that cultures around the world have in common. There are others, like the Adam and Eve story, whose characters bear various names, and also stories about good and evil and Godlike men who were referred to as the brilliant or shining ones. I often wondered why we were kept in the dark about some of the things written in what is supposed to be sacred scriptures. If it really is "sacred," then why hide it from people or omit it from the education curriculum? Must we continue to live in the dark? In my mind, sacred knowledge must be shared so that all may be enlightened. Equally important is the fact that all knowledge is sacred!

Have you ever read any of the old religious texts or taken a college course on world religions? It's OK if you haven't because I can sum up what you would have learned in a few words— extremely confusing and mostly unlikely, if not completely unbelievable. What I did observe about the so-called religions of the world is a trend toward repetition. Each new religion seems to have parallels with religions that came before. The main characters and events seem to be based on characters and events from earlier religious texts. I can only imagine how this could be applied to a time in the very distant past before writing was a thing. Over time, clans would grow and splinter off, going their separate ways. As various cultures developed, they would retell the same basic story with their own twists on it and with character names familiar to themselves.

I no longer think about this topic in the time frame of the ancient Greeks, Romans, Celts, and so on, but very much earlier, historically speaking. I even think of what might have been happening in prehistory, a time before the Sumerians and Dravidians even began recording events. Much evidence has emerged in recent years that contradicts much of what is written in our scholarly texts and shows us that the world of six thousand years ago was actually a complex mix of cultures intertwined through trade and travel over vast distances. It seems we behaved then much as we do today.

As a side note, hopefully the next generation of textbooks for our children will be more factual and not as politically dictated as they are now. I am sorry if this offends anyone, but I almost have to laugh when I read about a Spanish, Italian, or Viking explorer discovering "this country" or "that land," and even though it is now evident that the Vikings visited North America a thousand years ago, they simply found a place that was already inhabited. We must start being more truthful about our past and start providing our children with the facts we know, regardless of the pressure to be politically correct. Give the explorers credit for their accomplishments (and failures), but let's stop making shit up and passing it on as history. Our children deserve better.

Humans are almost everywhere these days, and there are all kinds of out-of-Africa and out-of-Asia theories. We can actually say now, with some certainty, where we were coming from twelve thousand years ago. Using modern DNA techniques, scientists now have a better understanding of the many human migrations that were driven by changing environmental conditions over time. We do know for certain now that we were not the knuckle-dragging, inarticulate idiots as some would characterize humans of a hundred thousand years ago. I know it is hard to believe, but about twelve thousand years ago, humans were already living in a civilized manner. Because of the recent archaeological activity in Turkey and elsewhere, we now know that a sophisticated and talented society existed in the region of the world known as the Levant, where present-day Turkey exists. If you would like to know more about this particular site, just Google it or open YouTube and search for information on *Gobekli Tepe.* In Turkish, it means something like "pot belly hill." It was thought for ages to be a natural hill, but alas, such wonders were hidden there. It is a great starting point for those interested in our mysterious past. Be prepared to be amazed at what was and what still is being found there. Many similar sites have recently been discovered in that area, and the truth is changing our history. The oldest excavated layers date to about 9000 to 9500 BCE. As work continues, I expect to see older dates.

Gobekli Tepe, Turkey

It is very logical to reason that if these complex and artistic sites were being built by humans, then our organizational and communication skills must have been highly developed already, and if the builders were not writing at that time, then their histories must have been passed on orally. Also, if we were building monuments and carving stone sculptures with real-life detail, we must already have been human in every sense. Also, because of the amount of planning and the human resources that were required, we must have been quite civilized by then as well. So, if we were civilized enough to build complex monuments like those found at Gobekli Tepe, then why did it take so long to start writing things down six thousand years later? It is almost as if there was no need at all to write things down twelve thousand years ago. Did we communicate telepathically? Maybe there were not enough people to bother ourselves with the need to record things. I find that doubtful as well. There is definitely a disconnect here that requires more information to understand. Hopefully in the next few years, we will finally get to see the whole picture after a huge ancient library or other source of information is recovered by archeologists.

Can we even say when we became human in the first place? You can bet it was a lot farther back in time than twelve or thirteen thousand years ago. Keep in mind that, just because we were human, it doesn't mean that we were Godlike yet. In a cave at a place called Denisova, in Siberia, archaeologists recently found bone and stone jewelry that shocked modern scientists. The bone belongs to a distant cousin of ours and was given the name *Homo denisova* after the name of the location where it was found. Amazingly, jewelry was found in strata dating to about forty thousand years ago. The Denisovans walked the Earth until about fifteen thousand years ago and interbred with our species, Homo sapiens, as did the Neanderthals. Analysis of the young woman's finger bone that was unearthed in the Denisova cave revealed that her parents were mixed breed, so to speak. If I remember correctly, her father was Denisovan and her mother was Neanderthal. When we read religious texts that say the gods created people in their image, were they even talking about us, Homo sapiens? Now I have to wonder at what point in time we were actually "made" or "enlightened," as some believe is a better translation.

It gets even more confusing when you consider the very word *human*. Were Homo neanderthalensis and Homo denisova human, or does that term apply only to us, Homo sapiens? Makes you wonder! It is obvious since we are the only humans left on the planet that nature gave us an advantage over all other hominids. Was it really just some natural fluke or luck that we prevailed, or is there more to the story? The very fact that such a beautiful artifact had been fashioned by a hominid forty thousand years ago is just mind-boggling. It really makes me wonder about the possibility that civilizations came and went much further back in time than we know. Only time and new discoveries will enlighten us about this possibility.

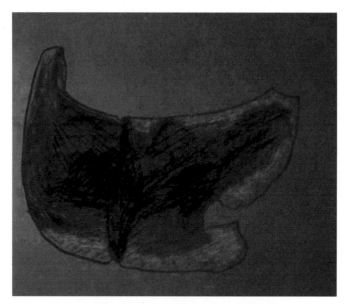

<u>Denisovan Bracelet: Illustration by Author</u>

Well, what did the gods do to us that would make us like them in some way thousands of years ago, and what makes us human in the first place?

CHAPTER

Human–What Are We?

W hat are we? The certainty of what we are and how we got here is a puzzle too complex for mere mortals to solve. We can describe ourselves quite elegantly and with a certain level of precision if we stick to a macroscopic view of ourselves. We can compare our stature and internal structure with other similar mammals and differentiate characteristics, but that is about all we can know. Once we start looking into our chemical and subatomic structure, we find that we are no different than anything else on the planet that possesses the same chemicals and elements as we do. This includes inorganic things as well, such as rocks, air, and water. There is one thing, however, that sets us apart from all other things in the universe— we are a marvelous creation and possibly the only life on the planet with a mind so sophisticated that we are endowed with the most important attribute of all— a free will.

The term "*man*" can be traced back to the Old English word "*mann*", referring to a person or humankind in general. The Old English "*mann*" can be traced back to the Ancient Sanskrit word "*manu*", which expresses "father of man." In Western religions, this would perhaps be something akin to Adam, the first man. Other cultures have their own names for the manu of their cultures. I believe this Sanskrit word goes back more than 3,500 years (1,500 BCE). The stories being written about at that time, however, were likely thousands of years older, if not more, having been passed down orally through the ages. You have to admit that it seems quite peculiar that humankind may have been evolving for millions of years, and then almost overnight, we were writing and building towns and cities. How is this possible, or is it all just a misunderstanding because of the lack of evidence?

So far, we have established that long, long ago, we referred to ourselves as "man" in the context of humankind. This fits with the logic that since this root word is common to many languages, it is likely a word passed down from antiquity via oral tradition many thousands of years ago. If this word has been in use that long, and if the gods created people, it must have happened at least as far back in time as the word has been used. This line of logic, however flawed you may find it, sets our "making" or "creation," as some have translated it, to some distant time, possibly around the time of the Younger Dryas period. In actuality, it could have been a vastly more distant time in the past for two reasons. First, geologists and climatologists know that the ice melt that accompanied the Younger Dryas period was but one of many found in the geological record. Second, archaeological records (Egyptian kings list) tell us of god-kings upon the Earth hundreds of thousands of years ago. So, our making by the gods could have occurred that far back in time. I hate to ruin a good story, but we still cannot put a fix on exactly when the gods actually created people in their image. Fitting the pieces of the puzzle together, with a few pieces— no, make that many pieces— missing, leaves us with a likely time sometime before the Younger Dryas when we were made or created or enlightened. The strongest evidence for this is the discoveries in Turkey at Gobekli Tepe and other related sites.

It is totally plausible that creation stories were just a means to an end as people tried to understand their origins. We have known for many generations that we, Homo sapiens, are the only remaining humans on the planet. However, I really would not be surprised if a variant of us was discovered in some secret remote wilderness hidden somewhere on the planet. We also know that during the Younger Dryas period, we lived alongside at least two other species of human: the Neanderthals (Homo neanderthalensis) and the Denisovans (Homo denisova). It is possible, if not likely, that other hominids were present as well. We also now know from DNA sequencing that some modern humans have traces of DNA from both the Neanderthals and Denisovans, which means that interbreeding occurred. The clues in our DNA show us that we are descendants of these earlier humans and, if not for their cunning and strength, we might not be here today. This speaks volumes about their level of intelligence and determination to survive in the face of possible planet-wide annihilation during the Younger Dryas and similar climate cycles in prior times. Will we be so lucky when the next ice age comes around? So far, no direct evidence supports the premise that there was a large human population on the planet prior to the last ice age, but we were here. Just when you think you might be able to make some sense of all of this, more confusion looms. It seems that we may be way more ancient than we have given ourselves credit for.

The fossil record shows us that there have been many upright-walking hominids similar to us for some three million years. It is very likely that these first upright-walking hominids had a natural push from living in the canopy to being knuckle-dragging landlubbers as a result of environmental pressures. We began using stone tools at about the same time. We must have been intelligent early on, and we must have understood the concept of time— perhaps not as we understand time today, but at least as it related to the natural cycle occurring in the everyday life of hominids a few million years ago. If protohumans waited until they were hungry to decide to forage or hunt for food, they likely would not have lived very long. Their understanding of time on a day-to-day basis was critical in the struggle to survive. You wouldn't want to go to the watering hole when the saber-toothed tiger was quenching its thirst each evening, but you would want to know the schedule that your favorite dinner animal keeps. We are not the only creatures of habit, and recognizing that fact has been advantageous for humanity. Further evidence shows us that early humans had knowledge of food sources at ground level and they even knew about the value of bone marrow. These humans were already intelligent enough to adapt to changing conditions and to find the necessary clothes in the form of hides to protect themselves from the environment. If humanity was intelligent enough to accomplish those things, then they also might have been able to communicate using a language of some complexity, even a million years ago.

There is a bit of a mystery surrounding what we were then and how we became what we are now. At some point in time, we suddenly became very organized and our numbers exploded. It seems that truth is stranger than fiction, but just what was the catalyst? Some scientists believe that it all comes down to changes in our environment that caused us to suddenly change our behaviors and create civilization. Others quote the Bible, which says that the Gods did it. Scriptures say, "the Gods created us in Their image …" Yeah, that is not a typo. Whatever the reason, we know what we are today on the macro scale. What we don't know is what changed us near the end of the Younger Dryas, about twelve thousand years ago. Did some god visit us from above and reveal to us the secrets of agriculture, animal domestication, and civilization? Could this have been the God of Abraham, "El," or the god of the Sumerians, "Enki," or perhaps even the force of the Hindu, "Brahman"? I have to admit that I am very much in tune with the Hindu theory of values, whereas I feel a Brahman connection to nature— that is to say, all things living and nonliving. I affect all things and all things affect me; therefore, my well-being is very connected to my relationships with everything in the universe.

By the way, if you read just a little bit about each of these religions, you may notice some similarities and a lot of differences. It is the similarities that catch my attention, and I can't help but wonder again if they are not all connected in some way in our very distant past. Is it even remotely possible that the planet we live on was being visited by travelers from the cosmos that were perceived as gods by early humans? Various cultures around the world have similar threads in their religious stories, and equally important, there remains physical evidence of a great civilization that spread common knowledge around the world. So, just how trustworthy are the ancient scriptures about the origin of humankind? I must clarify that the only documents I feel worthy of inclusion in a discussion about religious texts are those referred to as the first five books of the Old Testament and some others that were deliberately omitted from the canon of sacred scripture by men who thought they were more informed than God.

I have come to understand that modern religion dictated by people is unnatural and a tool to use over those who cannot master their own thoughts. Anything considered religious in nature that was written after about 50 BCE is complete trash in my opinion, even if some of it may be based on actual facts. I believe there may be some facts in the later writings based on ancient stories, but not enough to be relied on as whole truth because of the massive amount of fiction that surrounds them. On the other hand, the ancient stories of the Old Testament seem to relate to a time when the Earth really was a smaller place and in which all cultures were interconnected to a common culture much farther back in time. It is because many myths and stories from prehistory appear common to multiple cultures that I place more credence in the ancient writings. I have no credence at all about stories invented by modern religious or political institutions. I do not need a human intervening on my behalf to tell me what I should or should not believe. I most certainly do not require the advice of others about my moral standards, and neither should you.

Another reason to have some trust in the older scriptures is because there is physical evidence all around the planet in the form of megalithic structures that have uncanny similarities. No one alive today has any knowledge as to who the builders were, and nothing has ever been found in the form of historical or archaeological finds that mention anything about all of those structures. They appear to predate even the Sumerian civilization. It is as if they were constructed in a time long before writing was a thing, perhaps so far in the past that even oral history has lost the details on when and by whom they were created. As far as I know, not one single culture or society on planet Earth can say who created them. I will discuss more on megalithic structures in a later chapter.

So, where does this idea about the gods making humankind in their image originate? It seems obvious to me that this idea was passed down orally in deep antiquity and later became a part of the Bible, known as the Old Testament. The first five books in the Old Testament are Genesis, Exodus, Leviticus, Numbers, and Deuteronomy. Collectively, the five books are referred to as the Pentateuch. It is here that we find the first mention of people being made in the image of the gods. Also, keep in mind that these writings echo the stories traceable to the Sumerians and Assyrians a thousand years earlier. Those earlier stories, in turn, were passed down through oral tradition for countless generations. To date, we have not uncovered a single document or artifact that points to the actual time in history or prehistory when humans were thus altered. Keep that point in mind as you continue reading.

As I mentioned earlier, it is very difficult to know what was originally meant by the expression "In our image." Yes, you read that correctly. It reads something like, "Let us make humans in our image, after our likeness, and give them dominion over the …". This is very controversial even today, as you can imagine. I went to Catholic school, and I was never told that there was more than one God. I wonder why. Many readers will accept this as nonsense and throw this book in the trash, but before you do, I suggest you get off your lazy butt and read the Bible for yourself rather than to trust others to interpret it for you. If you don't have a copy of the Torah, Koran, or Bible lying around the house somewhere, just Google it. Some scholars believe the plural translation "Gods" is a flawed translation of Sumerian to Hebrew that occurred sometime in the distant past, but most believe it to be accurate. Aside from that, the oral traditions were still alive and in use at the time this subject matter was first written down. After all, oral tradition was the very source of the stories. It is not likely, in my opinion, that both methods of communication would be misunderstood in exactly the same way. Remember, about a thousand years before the Torah was compiled, clay tablets were being created that tell us, virtually, the same story.

To this day, debates rage about what God is and what it means to have been made in God's image. I cannot tell you what to believe, but know this— you have not been told everything, and as a species, we are born ignorant and we are very lazy by nature. Being lazy with our minds does not make things any easier for us, either. Whoever— or whatever— our Creator is, we were given great tools to work with to be self-sufficient, intelligent, and of a free will. It may have taken several thousand years for our transformation, or it could have been just a few generations of genetic manipulation, but compared to what we were three million years ago, we (humans) are now as gods upon this Earth. Just think about this for a minute. If you believe the ancient texts and take them even slightly serious, then you should realize that in "their" image, you were created, and therefore, you were given the intelligence to make your own decisions. Pick up any Bible and you will see this in Genesis as it was written five thousand years ago and as it was likely spoken in a much greater antiquity.

We are, therefore, nothing more than the craftsmanship of the gods who created us in their image. It is almost impossible for us today to precisely grasp the meaning of being made in *their* image! Likewise, it would be futile to argue about whether there is a literal meaning to the phrase "create humans in our image." We need to understand only that, in deep antiquity, humankind was repeating stories down through the generations about events that were important enough to be remembered and passed on. What is most interesting to me is the amazing story of why we were made in their image. I expect I will not live long enough to share in the discovery of the ancient knowledge that will reveal exactly when this event occurred, but the Sumerian accounts of what occurred point to people being made solely for the purpose of serving the gods. It really is literally written in stone. When I write *God* with a capital G, it is to make the point that people were created to be subservient to their Creator. This was objective, upfront, and personal, however cruel it may seem to us now. It appears our only purpose was to be a labor force in servitude. Wait— isn't that pretty much how modern religions use us? It actually looks as if we were just stone-aged hunter-gatherers who were modified to fit the needs of the gods. That modification may simply have been in the form of an education that permitted us to live as the gods lived, that is to say, in a civilized and cultured society. Much more research is needed along these lines.

Two Gods Anointing a King (?)

I have often wondered about the possibility that people, at some point, might have suddenly begun to question how they became what they saw themselves as. I can imagine a newly awakened mind pondering the creation of the first of its kind. I can even imagine the first person creating his or her first gods to explain the unexplained in his or her natural surroundings. What I cannot imagine is how people would come to pass down these incredible stories about the gods with such specific details about their purposes here on Earth and their purposes for creating people. It is just unimaginable to me that a hunter-gatherer sat by the fire ten or twenty thousand years ago and decided to make up a story about how he or she was created. My take on this is that when the gods made us in their image, we were just slaves to be molded, nurtured, and eventually given the ability to procreate in good numbers to maintain a living workforce. I also believe that making us in their image refers to altering our genetics in such a way as to produce a workforce that could comprehend complex instructions along with the communication skills required for the tasks expected of us. I do not believe it refers to cloning us, but I can't prove otherwise.

According to the ancient texts, we were given the tasks that the minor gods grew tired and weary of. It seems they could no longer bear the chores of working the gold mines. Now you might be asking, "OK, that's a joke— right?" Remember that I said the truth is stranger than fiction. Actually, the Sumerian story is literally written in stone. No one knows what our condition was prior to our transformation, but after the gods were done making us, we were pretty much what we are today. Possibly one side effect of being made in their image is that we developed a free will, which is a double-edged sword in every way. On the one hand, you could choose to do what you were told; but on the other hand, to refuse would likely have meant death. Sounds familiar, does it not? Keep in mind that our transformation may have taken a long time to come to fruition for the gods, but then again, as attested to in the kings list, the ancient ones had an incredibly long lifespan. I am talking tens of thousands of years each. This information is found in both Egyptian and Sumerian writings. Even the later modern religious texts talk of life spans of many hundreds of years. When I discuss the man-gods of old in a later chapter, I will revisit this topic. So, that is what people are, in my humble opinion. A human is nothing more than just a hominid who was modified to fit the needs of the gods. That is also what differentiates people from all other creatures. You can choose to use your own mind or you can choose to be led like sheep. You can choose to listen to gossip and supposition, or you can choose to seek out the truth in all things. You can choose to vegetate or choose to learn and improve yourself. You can give up hope, or you can choose to fight to improve your condition. Yes, you really can change the environment in which you live, sometimes simply by leaving it behind. You can choose to stay lost, or you can seek guidance from those known to effectively assist others in related circumstances. To do nothing is not an option! To think critically is to think like a god.

I have heard many people speak about leaders and followers. It used to be understood that leaders give orders and that followers follow orders. In most cultures, it was also understood that leadership and dominance went hand-in-hand. Male dominance prevailed in most cultures throughout human history. However, the trends are changing rapidly. Dominance and leadership are more tightly coupled to intelligence these days than to brute force. It appears that the rule of law is finally overcoming some of the bias baggage of the past. I am certain this is directly related to the increased levels of literacy and education in general around the world. The reason I discuss this here is that we must understand that our status on the planet is not static or fixed. We are a complex and dynamic mixture of hominids who must strive to better ourselves if we are to maintain the gift of the gods within ourselves.

Sometimes I believe I am witnessing the dimming of the light in the minds of many people around the world, and it is terrifying to think where we are headed as a species if this continues. I see education as an important tool in ensuring the longevity of humankind. It does not require a great stretch of the imagination to understand that some portions of the population are failing in this endeavor. Within the laws of our societies, we must do all we can to ensure that each one of us has the opportunity to improve his or her life, both physically and spiritually. As I have witnessed over the last half of the twentieth century and into the twenty-first century, many of the people I have known were not willing to challenge themselves to learn more, to achieve more, or to improve.

According to the ancient writings, the gods, at one point in time, chose not to walk with humanity any longer and then left humankind with a lifespan of 120 years. For me, it seems there should be no reason to believe that striving to be godlike should not be on everyone's agenda. I truly believe that by making humans in the image of the gods, we were given superior intelligence, the ability to think critically, and, most importantly, a free will to chart our own destinies. This is the humanity we are today. Since we have the ability to better ourselves, we really need to be more proactive in choosing our paths through life. Bettering ourselves and our children may be easier than you might first imagine. The key is, of course, education. We need to begin the healing process and to start turning on the lights so that everyone can see the facts. We must fight to ensure that our children are educated with the current facts. We must teach them to use their minds and to think about all things critically. They must learn how to question the status quo. Yes, it is OK to question authority, but it must be done in a respectful manner and remain within the confines of the law at all times. The education I am thinking of is not limited to schooling on a governmental level. It must start much earlier than that. I will touch on this topic in more detail in a later chapter because it really is relevant. In the meantime, perhaps we should try to understand our Creator as well as the God of Abram (Abraham) in the Old Testament scriptures.

CHAPTER

God—Who or What Are You?

So, what is our real history, and what exactly are we talking about when we use the word *god*? To be sure, the term *god* does not necessarily mean the same thing to others as it does to you. The mental picture you have is determined mostly by your upbringing and your acquired paradigms. Every child is brainwashed while growing because he or she has no choice but to believe everything they are told by elders and trusted members of society. This is simply the result of the need to survive. Are the myths about the Norse gods, like Thor and Odin, or the Greek gods, like Zeus and Poseidon, just fables, or did there actually exist a group of gods that walked the Earth alongside humanity? I am sure that the children of those societies believed without a doubt that the stories were fact and not just fiction. Indian culture has parallel stories of gods, such as Shiva and Vishnu and many other lesser gods. The people of the Americas also worshiped a plethora of gods prior to the advent of Christianity, and many still share allegiance with both the old gods and the new ones as well. The truth is that most Christian rituals have some connection to pagan practices of the past. A whole series of books could be written on that subject alone.

God-King on Winged Chariot

Everyone has a different take on what the term *God* means. To some people, God is a benevolent being that exists somewhere in the cosmos, protecting those who choose to believe and granting the believers eternal happiness after death. Others say that God is an imaginary figure that people use to explain things in the universe that they cannot understand. Even others say that it is wrong or forbidden to question what God is at all. I, personally, never was very good at blindly believing everything I was told. In reality, I don't think it matters what you believe as long as your seek the truth about the world around you and how you are connected to it and to the universe. If you are honest with yourself and search passionately for the truth in all things, eventually you will come to understand yourself, after which, all things become transparent. It will then be very difficult for the people you trust to blindly lead you through a meaningless life without fulfillment. You will no longer be just another hypocrite. You will decide what your moral ground looks like, and you will lead instead of follow. We must remember that religion in deep antiquity was mostly about relating to and respecting the natural world around us. Some cultures still follow this practice, even today. It could be as simple as routinely looking at the night sky in awe of its beauty or celebrating and showing thanks every year when the days start getting longer again. As a side note, I am always thankful when December 21 arrives each year. As soon as I know that the days are getting longer again each day, I feel a renewed energy that helps me fight through the long and cold winter nights. I anticipate the warm spring days that will follow. In fact, I honestly believe that the so-called pagans of old got a really bad rap. It seems that they were much more in touch with nature than most of the religious folks of today's modern societies.

As you can imagine, early humans may have had more than one god to thank or to be angry with. On a good day, people may have been thankful for the warm sunshine and may have shown their thanks by praising the sun as it disappeared below the western horizon. Perhaps, at some point in time, the absence of a thankful gesture at sunset would have been seen as jeopardizing the morning arrival of the sun in the eastern sky on the following day. We may never know when or what made people begin to associate objects in nature with gods, but we do know that five thousand years ago, a plethora of gods were being worshiped by every known culture. Many indigenous cultures around the world still practice some degree of animism, whereas all things like people, trees, rocks, mountains, animals, and so on possess their own individual spirits or souls. The Hopi culture, which sadly enough was forced onto a reservation (another book there) that is quite small and is itself located within another much larger reservation in Arizona in the United States, have religious beliefs along these lines. They also believe in a higher power or intelligence responsible for creating all things, but this is not to be equated with the God of Abraham or other modern religions.

More and more researchers and scientists are finding evidence of a cosmic energy that is pervasive throughout the universe. Some are suggesting that even what they thought of as the smallest particles are actually not particles at all, but energy fields of extremely high frequency confined to an unimaginably small point in three-dimensional space. Wrap your head around that! Discoveries like those actually add credence to the practice of pantheism, where all things are connected to a common force (soul) rather than having an independent or individual soul, as in animism. "May the Force be with you!" I do not believe our species will survive long enough to ever discover the Creator of the universe. I do believe, however, that we must continue to expand our knowledge in every way possible. Who knows? Maybe we will figure out how not to destroy ourselves. The scriptures relate to a God who is all knowing. If the gods made us in their image, then perhaps we should also strive to be all knowing.

Let's take a closer look at what we mean when we say *God* or *gods*. The God who chose Abraham and his family to follow and worship Him is the God of today's Jewish, Christian, and Islamic scriptures. It just does not make much sense to me to equate the God of Abraham with the Creator of the universe. I really believe there is a mistranslation or mistransliteration of the term for God that has caused two different original thoughts to be merged into one. Just think about it for a moment. The God of biblical scriptures is vengeful and cruel. This God also always has people do his bidding for human events. However, the Creator of the universe has no more regard for humankind than for any other living organism on Earth or elsewhere. The laws of the universe are set in motion— job done. There are no demands on humankind and no need to interfere with the progress of human evolution.

If you are surprised that I state that the God of the Bible is cruel and vengeful, then you obviously have never read the Bible. I am not a Bible scholar by any means, but I was forced to read it as a child in school. I began to read it more thoroughly throughout my early years, especially when taking certain college courses, and that gave me reason to reflect on and question what I was taught as a child. One of the most shocking stories in the Bible for me was about how God ordered the killing of men, women, and children in 1 Samuel 15. When read critically, one can easily see that all is not what it seems. For being such a short story, as it is, there is plenty of evidence that the Creator of the universe had nothing to do with it. In modern legal terms, it is all hearsay. Someone said that someone said such and such. Why would God have to tell Samuel to go and tell Saul to kill all of the Amalekites? Read the previous sentence again or, better yet, read the scripture for yourself. I guess it was the same reason that God had to tell Samuel to tell Saul that he (God) appointed him (Saul) to be the new king of Israel.

Was Samuel able to speak the same language as God but Saul was not? Why did God not remove the unholy people himself? This whole story smacks of political intrigue. It even seems as if Saul was being appointed king because God was not up to the task any longer. He couldn't even tell Saul what he wanted without an intermediary like Samuel. Seriously, it seems as if Samuel was literally used as a translator. Oh, by the way, this is not a one-off in the Bible. Could the power of the God-king of that region have begun to wane? Was time and age taking a toll on one of the last man-gods on the planet? Can you imagine the Creator of all things, an omnipotent and all-knowing God, who needed a translator to get a message across? I am not falling for that! What else can scripture and ancient stone writings tell us about the gods of old?

Men Following Their Lord's Wishes to Wage War

According to ancient writings, in antiquity, the god-kings possessed instruments or machines of great power that commanded fear and respect. This very much sounds like a story of a god-king who had been forced to relinquish the power of kingship to a human counterpart just to survive. Even if you are not religious, please take an hour or two and try to read some of the Bible stories and you will better understand what I mean when I infer that the God of the Bible was actually a man-god and maybe even the last to walk our planet. There are other similar examples of this type of behavior, and always, the God of the Bible is using humans to intervene on His behalf. Another clear example of God's inability to interact directly with humans is found in the writings about Ezekiel. Even as the God of the scriptures was unable to speak or otherwise communicate with the various tribes, apparently Ezekiel had no problem. Also keep in mind that the God of Abraham may not have been alone on the planet, but likely was one of the last. The God of Abraham (approx. 2000–1500 BCE) and the God of Ezekiel (approx. 590 BCE) may indeed have been two different entities. Although the timeline for Ezekiel is considered to be fairly accurate, the true timeline for Abraham, if such a person actually existed, is much more uncertain.

What I am implying here is that different regions or areas of population may have had their own war-lords controlling those regions. There are similar stories of gods controlling the human population in other parts of the world, as well. The ancient Vedic writings even tell of sky battles between the gods. Then something occurred that crippled the powers of the god-kings. Perhaps it was then that kingship was handed down to humanity. To some people, several thousand years seems like a very long time, but don't forget that before we were made in the image of the gods we were probably still using stone tools. If you take some time to research the ancient kings list (please do it), you will see some confusing, but perhaps revealing information about the lifespans of the ancients. The god-kings ruled sometimes for thousands of years each. No wonder their original workforce got tired of mining for gold. Of course, one cannot take the dates literally as stated in the kings list. As the list goes on, the later kings were not living or ruling quite as long as their predecessors. This is a key point to consider, and we will discuss this further in a later chapter. If these god-kings were just interlopers, where is the real God who created the universe? You will never, ever, find the answer to that question! The question itself isn't even logical.

At some point in time, about six thousand years ago, we suddenly learned how to make metal tools. We used stone tools for over three million years, and then suddenly everything changed for humans. Was this the point that we were modified, or shall I say, made in the image of the gods? I find myself pondering two trains of thought at this juncture. First, I consider that we may have been mining gold for the gods for many thousands of years but were never permitted to use our knowledge freely for our own development. Believe me when I say that if you can melt and refine gold, then you can certainly work copper and iron as well. It is possible that a natural catastrophe reduced humanity to small numbers and that all of the old knowledge was lost, but no one has found any evidence of this being the case. Second, perhaps our enlightenment occurred in a very short period of time, say a dozen or so generations. This would be a better fit for the establishment of oral tradition that remained in the human story and was passed down until the advent of the written word.

The ancient stories tell of people receiving knowledge from the gods who taught them to farm, to write, and to build settlements. I do not believe the first settlements were large enough to be referred to as cities, but these stories may be telling us that the gods or their offspring were still on the planet rather recently, perhaps as recently as a few thousand years ago, and maybe later. I will expand on that thought later when I address some theories about giants. In either case, it seems that every god-king residing on Earth wanted to have his or her own sacred territory in which to erect a home as well as a temple for people to worship them locally. I must mention here that the ancients used words for God that can also be translated as *Lord*. Some Jewish scholars translate the term *Elohim*, which appears in ancient scriptures, as something akin to highest one(s) or Lord(s). To me, a lord is the same as a master. That makes perfect sense because the god-kings of antiquity ruled over the humans who were made in their image. Looking at things in a rather simplistic manner, maybe the God who spoke to Abraham was one of the god-kings who established his presence on Earth and used Abraham to grow his earthly kingdom, however long that took. If we take into consideration what the Bible says about Abraham's age, it seems he may even have been one of the offspring of the man-gods of antiquity. Breaking news! The gods controlling the humans began behaving badly at some point by disobeying the orders of the boss god. More about that later.

I believe a combination of new tools in our toolbox was the reason for our sudden increase in population. These tools included the ability to better organize ourselves, acquiring better interpersonal skills like language and social norms, having brain development that enabled us to better predict outcomes, and improving observational skills as well as other unknowns. It would appear as if our DNA had been edited to give us a leg up. We became destined to be the rulers of the planet, that is, to have "dominion over the fishes, the cattle, the fowl, and all things that creepeth upon the Earth."

Recent studies show that our DNA is not written in stone. It is, in fact, very dynamic. It can be changed over time because of stresses inflicted upon us by our environment. Some researchers believe we were modified using gene editing, but we will likely never be able to prove that case because of the length of time involved. Maybe, just maybe, it had nothing to do with any god at all. Although routine aberrations occur naturally, our DNA is capable of repairing many of these minor changes. Chronic stress at a young age, however, can cause changes that last a lifetime and can actually change gene expression in the brain. This is a real revelation. Could something have occurred six thousand to twelve thousand years ago that caused us to suddenly become more aware, more intelligent, and ingenious? Well, something happened, but the changes in behavior seem to be too varied to have been caused by just one natural catastrophe or Earth-shattering event. I have read, however, that it is common for traumatically stressed individuals to pass down genetic changes that occurred because of the stress, not just to their children, but to their grandchildren as well. This is a relatively new field of science known as transgenerational epigenetics. Now, that's some heavy stuff!

OK, so if the God of Abraham was one of these visitors, what's the timeline look like? Because humanity's collective memory speaks of gods who made us in their image and that our earliest written religious texts are from about five thousand years ago, and we now know that the same stories were likely handed down over many, many generations, the likely conclusion is that this was an actual event that occurred much earlier. Who the hell would have made up such a preposterous story six to twelve thousand years ago? In my opinion, there must be something to it. This is not an argument to prove one thing or another, but a simple conclusion based on what we know today— information we did not have even fifty years ago. The information keeps pouring in as more and more sites are unearthed. Now, with the quickly melting ice in Antarctica and elsewhere, we can expect our knowledge to rapidly increase. Sadly, we are already in a situation where we do not have enough serious-minded students to help translate the backlog of ancient writings that have already been collected. If you have or know students who enjoy ancient history, please nudge them toward a university that has an antiquities department. When the gods rewrote our DNA, they gave us a thirst for knowledge. As it implies in the religious texts, knowledge is the realm of the gods. Maybe we are becoming as gods just by the nature of our curiosity. Well, maybe some of us are. I say that because I see so many people who just can't be bothered with knowledge of any kind. They just want to let someone else do everything for them, and for that, they are more than willing to follow like sheep. Very sad indeed!

Most cultures in antiquity worshiped gods that they created in their desire to relate to their environments. There were storm gods, wind gods, sea gods, gods or goddesses of fertility, earth gods, fire gods, and so on. Lesser known are the man-gods of Genesis, the first book of the Old Testament. They are frequently referred to as giants among men. The Sumerians wrote of them, but we have no way of really knowing what their definition of a giant was. It is not likely that they were fifty feet tall or anything like that. They may have been much taller than the average person of that time, but many scholars believe that the term *giant* may have referred to a being who possessed great knowledge or power. Even today we refer to people who achieve great things as "giants in their fields." There are several accounts referring to giants in the ancient religious texts, and some scholars believe that those giants were the offspring of the gods who fell out of favor because they came down to mate with the human women on the planet. Yes, it is stranger than fiction. Again I ask, who would have thought up something like this over six thousand years ago if there was not some shred of evidence that it had actually occurred? Believe it or not, there is even more to this intervention than you might imagine. Not only do the ancient texts tell a story of visitors to planet Earth who parked above and sent workers and leaders to the surface to mine gold, but after some time, the workers decided this work was too difficult and asked for help from above. The gods made humans in their image and put them to work.

The earthbound gods were happy for a while until some of them suggested that they take the women of mankind and bear offspring with them. This was prohibited by the gods above and created a tense situation, and the gods upon the Earth were warned about this. They disobeyed and took for themselves what women they desired, and their offspring became half gods and half human. I could not have dreamed this up. It really is written in stone from so far back in time that the Old Testament was still over a thousand years in the future. The viable offspring were destined to be remembered as the demigods of old like those spoken of in the Greek and Norse fables. I strongly feel that there is enough textual evidence from cultures all around the world that there is some truth about the existence of demigods in the past, even if the information that remains has been totally corrupted. The point here is that multiple cultures separated by time and distance have this common thread. How else could a worldwide history of such events have been created thousands of years ago? More importantly— why?

Still a topic of hot scholarly debate is what really transpired. The children of this unholy union mentioned in scripture are referred to as the Nephilim, as translated from ancient Hebrew writings. There appears to be no consensus on exactly who or what the Nephilim actually were. What is interesting is that this occurred while Noah was alive, because it is at that time when one of the gods reveals to Noah the anger of the gods above and their desire to cleanse the Earth with a great flood. Now, I have to wonder if this is actually in the time of Noah or of a similar character thousands of years prior. Remember that much of what is written in the earliest Jewish scriptures has a prototype from ancient Sumeria, which in turn was passed down orally from an even more distant past. I place my bets on a more distant past, possibly many thousands of years before the time of Noah.

It is interesting to mention here that various biblical characters are noted to have had conversations with God or the gods of antiquity. It seems to me that there might just be more than one possibility that explains how people thousands of years apart could have spoken to the same god. The simple explanation is that there were many gods or god-kings present on the planet over exceedingly long periods. The ancient writings speak of visitors who worked the mines in the ages before humans were created. They were organized and had earthbound leadership, and eventually a kingship was created to control the population at each of the mining areas around the planet. These early kings were the god-kings of antiquity. These god-kings lived and ruled for thousands of years each. They certainly would have been feared and worshiped by early hominids, even before the creation of humankind. It is not unlikely that various hominids and their descendants were aware of the same god over a vast time span. Again, I refer you to the kings list to get an idea of how long some of them reigned. I do not believe someone made this stuff up just for the hell of it. Someone went through a lot of effort to put this writing in stone to secure it for posterity. Modern research indicates that the length of time that some of those kings ruled are greatly exaggerated. Also, it appears that some of them ruled simultaneously in various city-states rather than in sequence, as interpreted from the cuneiform translations. The big takeaway for me is simply that as time passes, they rule for shorter and shorter time periods.

As you can surmise, most people think of God as the God of Abraham and Noah (God of the Bible) but also mistakenly equate this God with the Creator of the cosmos. When they learn about God from the mouths of people, they learn that God is all powerful and all knowing, even though the Bible passages indicate otherwise. Really, if God was all knowing, why would he require human spies to check out the land of the Canaanites? At times, the texts seem to be contradictory. In one place, they speak of a kind and compassionate God, whereas at other times, these texts tell us that this God is very cruel indeed. This particular God or Lord from the Old Testament most certainly behaved in a manner reminiscent of a modern warlord! Today, in most modern societies, we would never blame a child for something a parent or grandparent did in the past, although we did just that a hundred years ago. It was acceptable to the ignorant masses likely because it was preached from "holy" texts by trusted church officials. Exodus 34 is a good example of the cruelty of a God who would punish the children of a sinner to the third and fourth generation. A sin can be anything that anyone of power can accuse you of. The Salem witch trials of the late seventeenth century are a perfect example. If you are not familiar with this historic event, please Google it to learn more. I am sickened at the thought that people can treat others with such malice and evil intent under the auspices of religion, yet I know it continues today.

Personally, I believe in nature. We must all find a way to be better humans and to educate ourselves and our children about our relationships with the environment around us. You can preach at me all day long that the Hopi and other indigenous cultures are pagans because they approach religion differently than the way the church thinks they should. I am OK with the Hopi and their beliefs because I know they are closer to nature for it. I think of God only as the Creator of the universe, and God's handiwork is what I like to refer to as nature. If nature and God are one, so be it. I am certain then that God is a woman— unpredictable, temperamental, and a provider of light and life. Perhaps that is why we call her Mother Nature! As for those poor souls who follow without thinking, if even one of them actually believed in the scriptures as being the Word of God, they most certainly would obey it— wouldn't they? If so, then why do they pray to statues and icons, which is explicitly forbidden by the Word of God?

Common Religious Idols from Around the World

Eventually, people were made in the image of the gods (not God, the Creator of the universe) and were given their role as worker bees. We were not made in the image of the universe; neither were the gods of antiquity all powerful and omnipotent. Let's keep Mother Nature and the gods who transformed us separate and distinct from one another. We do not know anything specific about the nature of the gods who created us. I find it quite interesting that the Old Testament tells of Moses receiving the Ten Commandments directly from God; however, Moses never was able to see God for all of those days he was on the mountain with Him. Also, when Moses asks God what His name was so he could tell his people, God gave a cryptic answer like, "I am that I am" and then says his name is YHWH (Yahweh). There may be other translations of this name, so I am sorry if I got it wrong. Also, there are many writings that refer to this God by the name *El*, but I do not know exactly where that comes from other than that the Hebrew word for Lord or High One is *Elohim* in the plural, as it appears in ancient Hebrew scripture. The point I would like to stress here is that this word or name (YHWH) is apparently not a word that Moses would be familiar with and appears to come from a completely foreign language. It is not Hebrew or Egyptian and may even have come from a language isolate. Is this another clue to visitors from above? Why do you think the God of Moses was afraid to show himself to a human that he was placing his trust in? Here's another question pertinent to this discussion. How is it that Moses was capable of understanding what God was saying if even his name (YHWH) was of a language Moses knew nothing about? I have to add here a rather odd translation about this meeting between Moses and God. Are you ready for this? The following is one translation of part of Exodus 19:16–20— "Now Mount Sinai was wrapped in smoke because the Lord had descended on it in fire. The smoke of it went up like the smoke of a kiln, and the whole mountain trembled greatly." That sounds just like a rocket landing to me! A similar event is recorded in the book of Ezekiel. Please read these stories to get a feel for just how wild they are. I might have dismissed them as myths if it wasn't for the amazing amount of details provided within the texts. On a side note, while researching Ezekiel, I learned that the original Hebrew scripture makes no mention of God in Ezekiel's writings, but later Bibles do, so is this really the Word of God?

Some researchers, based on stone carvings and pictorial writings as used by the Egyptians and other cultures, believe that the creatures that visited Earth and created humans were not exactly like us at all. Also, there is no physical evidence to suggest that this story is even true. Some researchers, however, have proposed various theories such as two-legged fish-like creatures or two-legged reptilians, but they have never found any real evidence of what they actually looked like. The Egyptian and Sumerian artwork is likely a rendering of oral history. In my opinion, making humans in their image had more to do with tweaking our intelligence and educating us rather than changing our appearance. Another line of thought is that we are physically identical in form and we are, in fact, the offspring and direct descendants of the gods that created us. We are the only remaining humans simply because our genetic tweaking gave us the advantage over all other species. Interestingly, the ancient writings also allude to two different classes of creatures (hominids?) that traveled down to the planet from above. One group was composed of the actual workers who physically worked the mines initially (Igiggi), and the other group had a higher status and were overseers to plan and execute the physical extraction of ores and manage society. It is possible that a third group existed who were not able travel down to the surface because of physical considerations. These high commanders were of the highest class, and it is possible that this structured society they brought with them may be the very reason why humans today have a tendency to place each other somewhere within a social class, even if only on a subconscious level. This also explains our willingness to be subservient to a God.

Keep in mind that other religions have their own takes on the idea of God or a Creator force that brought all things into existence. What is most interesting to me is how various cultures make use of their religious practices to maintain control over the population in general. In many cultures, religion and politics are comingled, even today. The best example of that is, of course, Islam. Perhaps someday soon, people everywhere will be permitted to choose exactly what their own consciences dictate, regardless of where they live. Can you imagine that?—Like the words of the John Lennon song— "Imagine." If you are not familiar with the song, I suggest you listen to it with an open mind and imagine for yourself what life was like before politics, wars, and religions were all being used to control people.

Now that we have a little better understanding of the term *God*, let's delve into how the man-gods came to be.

CHAPTER

Man-Gods—Legends of Old

Thor—God of Thunder

Poseidon—God of the Sea

If some people sat around a campfire and made up these stories just for the hell of it about ten thousand years ago, they must have had one hell of an imagination. Maybe it was the magic mushrooms they ate

32

for dinner! The ancient religious texts have several fantastic and unbelievable stories that just boggle the mind. The man-god stories are accompanied with other strange stories from antiquity, such as visitations from above by gods in flying machines and aerial battles with sky crafts shooting at one another with beams of great energy. Apparently, the earthbound gods of old did not get along well. They behaved a lot like modern warlords! Pure fantasy— right? Who created these fantastic stories, and most importantly, why? These stories are thousands of years old. How the hell could someone come up with this stuff back then when we have been flying for only a few hundred years, not to mention aerial warfare with lasers? Oh— wait a minute! Maybe we really did have a civilization in the past where all these things were possible. What if the man-gods who survived the flood or floods of antiquity found themselves without any god-bosses above to rule them? They would have been stranded and left to their own devices. Left behind with limited godly resources, they would have been keen to protect whatever craft and power sources that remained. Consider the rest of this chapter before writing off this possibility.

Studies of the ancient writings further reveal that, after many thousands of years, the earthbound gods grew weary and desperate for relief from the toil of working the mines. Even if they were just explorers who happened upon planet Earth, they would surely have been gods in the eyes of the indigenous hominids already existing on the planet. Humankind was created and was most certainly subservient to their maker. The details of how long it took and how many were made is not of significance, as we can only speculate without more hard evidence. What is written is that the god-kings, at a very specific point in time, suddenly decided to give kingship to people so that they could rule themselves under the guidance of the god-kings. Why would they do something like that? I have a theory that I believe is worth considering: perhaps it was just a matter of time.

As the human population grew, the god-kings likely spread out the workforce to where it was needed most. More people means fewer resources, generally speaking. They would have had an immense administrative responsibility to keep the workers happy and in good health. A sick or dead worker is not very productive. All of the workers' societal needs had to be met as well. The towns or cities that grew out of the areas surrounding the mines were established as religious communities (cults, if you want to call them that) with the god-king, the all-supreme, at the top of the pecking order. The king's immediate subordinates would be his fellow earthbound visitors who remained at his locale, either voluntarily or otherwise. They would gladly serve their king if it meant staying out of the mines, or at least not having to do the hard work anymore. Other god-kings in various locations around the planet would establish similar worship centers or communities for their subordinates to show their piety. For the mining centers and communities to survive, they needed all the trappings of a civilization, including water, sanitation, and food stores, as well as agriculture, government, and laws. They likely didn't have it all at the beginning, but they certainly had it all around 6000 BCE.

We do not have a full picture of why each location for a city or town was chosen where it was. Many physical changes have occurred in the landscape since the first towns were founded, therefore, many details that would have shed light on their beginnings have been lost to time. It is extremely likely that a source of fresh water was a primary prerequisite for a population center to be established. It may not be the only prerequisite, however, as some population centers may have been based solely on political or religious considerations. Perhaps needing a place to hide is a good reason for choosing a specific location. Consider a scenario where a powerful clan leader comes under threat from relatives or neighbors who are intent on taking the clan's resources, which may include people as well. The clan leader or king may choose to relocate to a more secure location that offers a higher degree of protection to grow his community. An ideal place would be one that is hidden from view or far off the established trade routes and perhaps even defensible by nature or the geology surrounding it. Even if water was scarce, canals and trenches that stretch for miles are not uncommon in the archaeological record.

But really, what compelled the sky gods to give up kingship and pass it down to the humans they had created? Well, first, not all of the earthbound visitors were on equal footing. There is no way that I know of to figure out exactly what was happening, but there was a level of stratification present from the very beginning. According to the ancient texts, two groups or classes of being were sent down to the planet— the god-kings and their worker-class servants, sometimes referred to as the Iggigi. Perhaps after living on planet Earth for extended periods, some natural conditions resulted in a reduction in the lifespans of these visitors, and they simply began to get older or weaker in health. I don't know about you, but my experience with getting older and doing hard physical labor adds up to lots of pain and discomfort.

The god-kings did not work hard, but perhaps life on the planet was a health risk nevertheless. This reduction in life expectancy is plain to see in the kings list as periods of kingship reduce over time. Again, ignore the actual numbers and follow the trend instead. This is also reflected in the lives of early biblical figures, which suggests to me that they may have, in fact, been demigods or children of the fallen ones. Yes, I am talking about the man-gods worshiped by various cultures around the world. In any case, for unknown reasons, there was also much intrigue and fighting among the god-kings either before or shortly after kingship was granted to humans. Perhaps, that is exactly what the fights were about. Ancient Indian documents mention flying crafts of various types in their Vedas and Hindu epics. Flying machines aside, the weapons of the gods were equally impressive with at least one that reads like a nuclear missile, where no blade of grass will grow for twelve years after it strikes an area, and the land is poisoned. Sound familiar?

Did someone really make that up thousands of years ago? Perhaps it is just fantasy translations by more modern scholars. Somehow, I feel something is going on here that is a little more than just pure fiction. In any case, the ancient writings from various cultures speak of great battles among the god-kings and of the long reign of some that lasted thousands of years. Of course, there were likely many factors involved, but eventually, kingship was delegated to a chosen few humans, or maybe half-human followers. Apparently, the god-kings could no longer function as in previous ages and chose to create worship cults to maintain their godly controls, not to mention their livelihoods. My take on the story of humans is that we were made in their image a few thousand years before the flood. It could have been much earlier, of course, and until we find more archaeological evidence, this will remain an open question. The last two god-kings of the kings list prior to the flood have reigns lasting twenty-one thousand years and eighteen thousand six hundred years, respectively. Then came the flood, after which, kingship descended from heaven, and the kingship was in Kish.

I believe what this is telling us is that, for possibly thousands of years before the flood, the god-kings ruled from a place in the sky (the heavens). Perhaps whatever caused the great flood was also a reason for the god-kings to leave orbit and abandon the earthbound god-kings. It is even feasible that the god-kings on Earth, or their offspring demigods, wanted to stay on the planet and revolted. The god-kings and their Igiggi underlings had taken human women and bore offspring that were half god and half human.

That was the cause for the flood in the first place, according to scripture. The story goes that the gods above wanted to destroy them all to cleanse the Earth of them and their abominable offspring. One of the earthbound gods, Enki, could not watch as all was destroyed, so he warned the humans of the impending disaster. Those who escaped went on to establish the earthbound kingships with god-kings ruling and, of course, fighting one another as soon as they became reestablished. According to the timeline of the kings list, the time from the great flood to the time when we can put a date on a king on that list is about eighteen thousand years. This would be the reign of Enmebaragesi, whose name is the earliest from the kings list to be attested to by archaeology. Keep in mind that new finds are always changing our knowledge, and this specific information may change at any time. He must have been a child or a recent generation grandchild of one of the fallen ones who had chosen to defy the boss gods by mating with a human woman. I say this because his reign is listed as having lasted nine hundred years. Note that this is much shorter in length than the god-kings reigning before the flood.

I have a suspicion that later generations of the god-kings lived shorter and shorter lives. Enmebaragesi reigned sometime around 2900 BCE. That dates the flood to around 21,000 BCE, or about twenty-three thousand years ago. The important note here is that by 2900 BCE, there were many competing city-states and conflict was common. As we mentioned, by this time, there were several cultures writing about battles between the gods, some with quite astounding detail concerning both the type of crafts they used and their peculiar weaponry. Keep in mind that these stories were most likely handed down orally for generations prior to being written down. For me, multiple cultures, vast distances, and similar stories equal a history lesson, however bizarre. So, if these postflood god-kings were children of the Nephilim, then they were, in fact, the man-gods of legend. Certainly, if you reigned for nine hundred years, simple humans would see you as a god and pass down stories of your great deeds over many generations.

Mayan Offering to a Man-god (War Lord?)

Prior to kingship being passed to humans, it is likely that people had no written language and may even have had a limited ability to communicate directly with a god-king, likely through a translator, such as one of the Iggigi. This may be the origin of the priestly class. Perhaps members of the priestly class were the direct descendants of the Igiggi who survived the flood thanks to the kindness of Enki, who warned of the coming deluge. There was a time in history when only special initiates were permitted to read and write because of the knowledge that could be acquired with such talents. Ignorance and submission go hand in hand! Of course, one could argue that people just made up stories to account for the natural phenomena they witnessed and endured. If so, then that points to the fact that some things recalled through oral tradition likely occurred in reality. Given that, it appears there were giants upon the land and "men of great renown," just as it is written down in ancient texts and modern scripture. Yes, this information is also in the Bible, the Koran, and the Torah. These modern scriptures all derive, in part, from the ancient writings of antiquity. One can be famous for many different reasons, and one can be considered a giant for various reasons as well. It appears from the wording in the ancient texts that some humans may have been more robust in features than other humans. Perhaps not all of them, but enough of them to make them as giants compared to the average Sumerian.

Genesis 6 clearly states that the Nephilim were on the Earth prior to and after the sons of God began taking human women as wives. Some researchers suggest that the Hebrew translation refers to the fallen ones or the ones who came down from above, but they cannot be the same as the ones who fell out of favor with the gods for taking human wives because they existed prior to that sin having occurred. It is likely that a subset, or a select group of the Nephilim were the ones who actually disobeyed their superiors in the heavens by taking human women for mates. On the other hand, the Nephilim may simply have been other hominids that were simply taller and more robust in stature. I know, it confuses me as well. In time, hopefully, enlightenment will come in the form of new archaeological and historical finds.

Genesis 6 further states that these Nephilim were "men of old, men of renown." My take on this particular verse is that the Nephilim were the last of the remaining Igiggi, who were some of the original, long-lived people from the stars, who, for whatever reason, were forced to remain on the planet. They were renowned for the fact that they had lived through the ages and likely possessed great knowledge and perhaps even retained mystical powers in the forms of technology that mere mortals could not conceive. Certainly any knowledge of medicine, chemistry, astronomy, botany, or any combination thereof, would make them gods among mortals. I remind you again that these great sages, the teachers of old, are not to be confused with the offspring of the union between the gods and women of humankind (demigods).

Although the Nephilim were great in many aspects, they were not kindly written about in later years when the Hebrews documented their stories. I believe that, over time, the oral tradition may have merged stories of the Nephilim with the stories of the giants who walked among humans in the time of Noah. In addition, I believe the Noah narrative to be a carryover of a more distant time many thousands of years prior. The term *giant* in the religious texts likely refers to a population group of early hominids who were physically robust and warlike. This could even be a reference to one of our distant human cousins, such as the Neanderthals, who were certainly much more robust and had the strength of several modern humans. If you think about Arnold Schwarzenegger and other famously strong people of the modern era, you can easily imagine the impression they would impart on anyone who had never met such a human before. Combine that with genetic traits that makes them much taller than the average humans of that time— and with a very aggressive nature— you get "giants." I can imagine these fearsome-looking, larger-than-life, uncivilized loudmouths pouncing on anybody just because they could. Hey, wait just a moment now. The truth is, most of this storyline is likely to be bullshit, especially if we are talking about the story of the spies that Moses sent to Canaan in preparation for taking the land from the inhabitants there as God (the warlord) had instructed. Keep in mind, God in this story is not the Creator of the universe and all things great and small. This is political intrigue at its finest. The history of events is usually written by the victors. Would you want to be remembered as a people who conquered shepherds or as a people who beat the odds and destroyed an army of giants?

David Defeats Goliath

The land of Canaan, referred to as "the land of milk and honey" in the Bible, covered a vast area. The many tribes therein may have had a united sense of belonging in a geographical sense, but there was no known central authority to which they all owed allegiance. They simply coexisted peacefully and likely bartered and traded goods and services throughout the land of Canaan and in lands afar. Yes, some of the tribes may have been scary-looking brutes, but it is not likely that all of the people of Canaan were of that nature. Most were just herders and tradespeople such as you would find today in similar rural areas. Once again, the scriptures present us with a God who requires humans to do his bidding. I told you— political intrigue. The God in this story is a Lord and possibly one of the last man-gods, improving his standing the only way possible— with aggression and a large army of followers. Are you seeing the trend here? We were made in their image to serve them as they see fit. They were selfish, aggressive, and warlike creatures that made us, and to this day we remain in their image. No wonder there can be little peace on this planet.

If you really think about it, all of the stories of myth and fantasy that speak of half-humans with god-like powers are quite similar. They can all do things that mere mortals cannot, such as commanding the elements like wind and lightning or having inhuman strength like Thor and his hammer that no mortal can lift. Some were simply wizards or magicians. Combining magic and a high level of education and intelligence can make any mortal seem like a god. Maybe King Arthur's Merlin was a real person, and maybe Moses did turn the Nile blood-red. It is one thing to simply tell generic stories about ancient heroes and quite another thing, indeed, to pass down or to put into writing the extremely detailed descriptions of people, places, and events that no human should have conceived of thousands of years ago. I joke about how some of the ancient writers must have eaten magic mushrooms or other hallucinogenic foods because it seems implausible that they could have been in a proper state of mind to have written those things in such detail unless perhaps there really is some truth in it after all.

There actually exists some ancient Hindu Sanskrit texts that tell of gods at war utilizing flying machines called Vimanas. They speak of various kinds that travel anyplace on the planet and even into the vastness of the solar system. Some texts tell of the Hindu god Shiva riding on a flying bird that was known for dropping bombs, and I am talking about real bombs that explode when they hit the ground, not the other kind. There is an uncanny resemblance in this Hindu epic to a passage in the Bible where Ezekiel describes his adventure surrounding a flying craft. He writes about seeing the Lord arrive and landing in a fiery craft that, among other things, had four very complicated wheels or wheel assemblies. The amount of detail in this account is what perplexes me the most. He describes a wheel assembly that can move in any direction without having to be turned. Is that even possible? Well, apparently so! NASA engineer Josef Blumrich (1913–2002) decided to design and patent an omnidirectional wheel based on the description in the Torah. Google it if you do not believe me. Let me ask you a question: Why would

God Almighty need a flying craft to come down to the planet to explain what he wanted humans to do for him if he is omnipotent and all knowing?

After learning about these things, the biggest question I have now is "where did all of those machines go, and why do we not have any physical evidence today?" I really hope I live long enough to see that question answered. Maybe it's true that "time heals all things". Maybe, just maybe, time also erases all things. Anyway, I really do get a whole new appreciation for the term *warlord* when I think about these stories. I could go on and bore you with more repetition, but I would like to think that won't be necessary. It is my hope that your curiosity is sufficiently piqued and that you will begin your own investigation into all of the information related herein. From sky-gods to the Creator, I have discussed various viewpoints that shed a little light on who is whom and what is what. Could it be that there is actually more physical evidence hiding in plain sight that adds some support for the actual presence of gods and giants living on our planet just as the ancient texts tell us? More important, why has this knowledge been swept under the rug and deliberately ignored, or do I really have to ask that question?

Just as the Catholic Church decided which books to exclude from the Bible in the fourth century AD, we are still being told what is truth and what is fiction by those who wish to control the narrative. Unless we try to turn on the lights, we will be destined to remain in the dark! Every day, in many places around the planet, many people see but choose to ignore what is in front of their eyes. I believe a combination of laziness of the mind and targeted distraction by mainstream scholastic institutions is the reason we are still being led down the path of ignorance. What if I told you that there are dozens of structures around the world that have uncanny similarities but were constructed many thousands of years ago? Perhaps we should investigate them, even if only superficially, to learn if any or all these sites add to the credence that a culture may have existed long ago on our planet. Not only that, but maybe giants existed as well. I am sure that it will surprise you just how much physical evidence remains.

It is no secret that many reports about so-called giants can be found simply by researching old news articles all around the world. My favorite story about red-haired, cannibalistic people of great stature comes from a place called Lovelock Cave, Nevada, in the United States. Spoiler alert: The current research indicates that any bones of the ancients retrieved from the cave have been lost to time; therefore, their size cannot be accurately determined. The Paiute people of the area still pass down stories of fighting and destroying a tribe of red-haired people who were cannibals. They do not mention giants in their stories, however, but recently bones were recovered from the cave that indicate the individual buried there was about 6'2". This is significantly taller than the average Paiute from centuries ago. If they were vicious and cannibalistic people, perhaps some would have seen them as giants or ogres, but nothing about giants is mentioned in their stories. It actually seems likely to me that almost every instance of modern-day talk of giants needs to be taken with a grain of salt. Even the biblical writings about giants who walked the Earth with people are likely referencing a different hominid species that had a larger build than other people of that time and place.

Now, it is time to start considering the real and tangible evidence.

CHAPTER

Physical Evidence—Pyramids, Ziggurats, and Caves

Perhaps this chapter will be the most interesting of all because it deals mostly with things that we can see and touch. If you make something out of stone— very, very large stone blocks, to be precise— it will last for a very, very long time. Likewise, if you craft an item of jewelry out of stone, it can remain intact for many thousands of years. It could last for forty thousand years or even longer. I would not say this if I did not already know of archaeological discoveries that date back that far. Some of the largest known stone structures are so old that it appears as if they must have been put in place by a lost, previous civilization.

Let's consider the timeline for modern humans. We have had electricity in our modern lives for only about two hundred years. About one thousand years ago, the Vikings sailed to the Americas and made contact with the aboriginal people there. Christianity is only about two thousand years old. Writing, farming, and city-building is only about seven thousand to twelve thousand years old, as far as we know. That being said, a most beautiful stone bracelet dated to about forty thousand years ago has been unearthed. It is clearly human-made. There appears to be some sort of time gap, where a sophisticated and talented society was kicked back into the Stone Age, pun intended! There are too many anomalies and coincidences in the archaeological record to ignore the fact that some of the things created and constructed in ancient times are all but impossible for us to replicate today, even with our modern machines and technology. I am not referring to jewelry here, but some of the massive structures found around the planet.

On a side note, any subject matter referenced herein can be independently researched by you, should you choose to accept the mission. Do not be afraid to uncover previously unknown information. Think critically about all you see and hear. Let no one tell you what to think or what to believe or disbelieve. Only you can prevent ignorance in your life. In most cases, a simple web search is all that is required for you to begin your quest for knowledge on any subject. For instance, you can do research concerning the forty-thousand-year-old bracelet that has recently been discovered. If you have access to a computer or a smart TV or phone, you can search for videos about said item using your favorite browser. You can even find videos on YouTube that cover the topic. When you get tired of reading, turn on the boob tube or your computer, but instead of watching braindead sitcoms, do some simple research that may open your eyes and shed a little light on all the lies you have been fed by the powers to be. Just remember to be critical in your thinking and try to validate all you see and hear. It is true— only you can prevent ignorance in your life!

When most people hear talk about ancient pyramids, Egypt is the first place that comes to mind. Of course, the reason for that is because ancient Egypt has been studied, talked about, written about, and is probably the most dug-up place in the world. Egypt, however, is not the only place where ancient pyramids were built. Almost everywhere around the world, one can find some sort of pyramid or pyramid-like human-made structure. It seems that, at some point in the past, pyramids were a status symbol like— I bet mine is bigger than yours!

The most interesting observation I have made is that there are ancient pyramids of various styles located in different parts of the world that are completely separated by time and are associated with apparently unrelated cultures. Once again, we have a clue of an earlier time when all cultures on the planet were building similar structures, which infers common knowledge. This is an example of the collective memory of a lost global civilization. At some point, this knowledge was known everywhere around the globe. The obvious question is, "What the hell were they used for?" To this day, Egyptian archaeologists still insist that pyramids are grand tombs for the pharaohs. To my knowledge, no mummies have ever been found inside of any of the Egyptian pyramids on the Giza plateau, so a critical thinker may come to other conclusions. Burials under a pyramid structure would make more sense and is expected since a pyramid is just an oversized mastaba. So, what are they? Hopefully, we will be able to answer that question soon as more and more pyramids are being found in countries that didn't even know they had them. The more we dig, the more we learn.

Great Pyramid at Giza, Egypt

Quetzalcoatl Pyramid at Puebla, Mexico

Although the famous Egyptian pyramids get the most attention, the Great Pyramid on the Giza plateau is not really the largest pyramid on Earth. The Great Pyramid of Khufu, possibly incorrectly attributed to Khufu, is the largest pyramid on the Giza plateau with an astounding volume of approximately 2.4 million cubic meters, covering about thirteen acres. However, there is an ancient pyramid sixty-three miles southeast of Mexico City that is about one-third larger in volume. The Quetzalcoatl Pyramid, located at Cholula de Rivadavia, has an approximate volume of 3.3 million cubic meters covering about forty-five acres. There are purported to be many more pyramids around the world, including in countries like China, Peru, Bosnia, Italy, Guatemala, Spain, and others. There are hundreds of smaller pyramids as well, such as the Nubian pyramids of Sudan, and even some pyramids that have been discovered under water. The main point here is that there are ancient pyramids all around the planet. There is some speculation that these structures were some sort of power-generating devices or perhaps communication devices to enable conversation between earthbound visitors and orbiting stations. I hope I live long enough to learn the truth about why they were actually constructed. My gut instinct tells me that the Giza pyramids were discovered by early Egyptian cultures, but constructed much, much earlier. I do not believe they were constructed as tombs, because any engineer intelligent enough to design and construct such a behemoth also would have known how easily a tomb raider could access and corrupt the tomb of any pharaoh laid to rest therein. Also, it is not likely that any one person had all the knowledge and responsibility of such a huge project. Many intelligent minds would surely be put to task on the project, and certainly at least one person would have seen it as a total folly to think the pharaoh placed therein would remain untouched forever.

My take on the pyramids, at least those at Giza, is that they were constructed for an unknown reason by an unknown culture and were later used by the Egyptians for rituals. Interestingly, the great pyramid of Khufu has recently yielded some interesting mathematical secrets. We will revisit this subject matter at a later point. Some of the tunnels and chambers may have been built in more recent times to make it look as though the structures were, in fact, hiding the body of a pharaoh and all of the riches that would normally accompany such a burial. As far as the so-called burial coffers found within, it is here that we find evidence of a technology that the Egyptians simply could not have had, in my opinion.

Please take some time away from your busy television-watching schedule and check out some YouTube videos on you smart TV or via the internet to learn more about the incredibly precise craftsmanship that went into the making of these massive granite boxes. I was not surprised to learn that no bodies were ever found in any of the precision-cut granite boxes. You may also find videos and documentaries about some of the other pyramids located around the planet. Try to keep away from the conspiracy theorists and only put stake in those who provide factual information without trying to sell you one idea or another. Remember to think critically. Whatever you do, avoid binge-watching the subject-matter videos. Too much at once will get you very confused and will interfere with your ability to think critically. Ideally, watching documentaries in a small-group setting would allow interested parties to critique and discuss the issues raised. Perhaps you can create a group of friends with similar interests to debate with after seeing a particular documentary. Search for agreement on specific issues and remember to agree to disagree without malice. Each person will come to a conclusion that he or she will have to live with. Believe in yourself and your ability to think critically. Don't expect anything to appear as purely black or white. Just try to reason what the most likely truth of the matter looks like.

Anyway, it appears that smooth-sided pyramid construction evolved from an earlier step-pyramid style. The step-pyramid style likely evolved from simple mastaba tombs that were large stacked-elevated platform structures. Each layer of block was smaller in area than the layer below it so that the outside surfaces resembled benches. *Mastaba* is, in fact, the Arabic word for bench. The burial chamber would have been located below the structure. One might conclude that if the older mastabas had burial chambers below ground, the later, larger pyramid structures might have the same configuration. Perhaps the chambers located near the center of the larger, more recent pyramids had a completely different purpose that we just have no knowledge of. Recently, many tunnels or passageways have been discovered beneath the pyramids on the Giza plateau. Mastaba tombs were in use over five thousand years ago. Where did the idea come from in the first place? As humans, we have always had a knack for copying the ingenuity of others. I surmise that a group of modern hominids found something strange in the shifting sands or perhaps perched high atop a mountain. The regular contours outlining the rectangular structure that they happened upon must have been quite curious indeed. Likely already thousands of years old, it certainly must have been placed there by an earlier civilization. There it was, and it was massive. What could have been the purpose of such a structure in the first place?

As you read more and more ancient literature, you get a sense that the gods who came down from the heavens did so in a craft that likely required some sort of level landing structure that could withstand the energy imparted as the crafts landed. Consider the Old Testament story of Moses meeting God on the mountain in the Sinai desert. In Exodus 19:16–20, we find a passage that sounds suspiciously like a rocket landing on the mountain. This is not as far-fetched as it might at first sound. Since there are these legends concerning sky-gods in various cultures around the planet, then it is no surprise that these structures are as common as they are. Could an ancient landing pad have been the inspiration for the design and building of mastabas or step pyramids everywhere around the planet? Just a thought!

Ancient Mastaba Ruins at Meidum, Egypt

Megalithic structures, other than pyramids, are found almost everywhere around the planet as well. A megalith is literally just a large stone (–*lith* means stone). If you do not think pyramids located around the planet in various locations is enough evidence to point to the probability of an ancient civilization, then we shall give you more. You could make a whole career out of just studying the megaliths on Earth. Can you even imagine people in ancient times picking up and moving a car or a bus or a train engine? The average weight of a car today is over a ton. A truck can weigh three tons, and a bus weighs about fourteen tons. How could they transport something that heavy? Well, someone did transport stone blocks at least that heavy in the distant past. What about a block of stone that weighs a hundred tons? What about seven hundred tons or more? That is so massive that I am sure we could not do it today even with all the equipment and technology at hand. That is why I believe our direct ancestors never did it; it was already in place. One particular structure that comes to mind is in Baalbek, Lebanon. Built by the Romans, the Temple of Jupiter is absolutely huge. Please create for yourself an opportunity to learn more about this amazing Roman feat of construction. Yet, the most important feature about this site is what the Romans did not do— or could not have done. I will not go into all of the reasons for this here, but it seems obvious to me that the Temple of Jupiter was built upon an already existing base. It looks as if the Romans found a marvel at the edges of their domain and were so impressed that they, as many had done before them, decided to build over the existing structure to claim it as their own. The foundation on which the Temple of Jupiter was built is huge in of itself. The site is on a natural slope and is therefore stabilized on three sides with walls of enormously heavy stone blocks. There are at least twenty-four huge blocks of stone weighing in excess of four hundred tons each. I do not believe that the Romans would have taken on this large of an engineering fete on the far edges of their empire as it simply was not necessary. As if four hundred ton blocks are not impressive enough, in one section of the wall, there are three blocks of limestone cut to fit perfectly straight and level, that are at least 750 tons each. The first thought I had when I learned of this was, "Why?" The Temple of Jupiter is a masterpiece of ingenuity and craftsmanship, but why would the Romans have made the effort to cut, transport, and position 750-ton blocks of limestone when four-hundred-ton blocks were fine everywhere else? That base was surely preexisting and had a long-lost purpose related to a long-lost culture. Again, we must give credit where and to whom it is due. The Temple of Jupiter is a masterpiece of Roman art, but I must note that the site itself is ancient, going back as far as 10,000 BCE according to historians and archaeologists. It is perfectly logical, then, to entertain the idea that the foundation may have been used for something entirely different many thousands of years ago. What purpose could such a massive structure have had back in antiquity?

Mastaba-Shaped Launch Pad

Note the mastaba-shaped launch pad at SpaceX. To me, the weirdest thing about megalithic structures is that they can be found almost everywhere. Megalithic walls can be found in Italy, Japan, South America, Greece, France, Russia, and elsewhere. I find the ruins located in Peru to be especially interesting. Some of the walls appear as interlocking jigsaw formations with curved or rounded corners, as if they had been in a semiliquid state at some point. They fit together so tightly, no mortar is required at all. Some researchers believe these structures were created with rock hammers and bronze chisels. I personally do not believe this conclusion at all. A notable feature found on many of these walls is that some of the blocks exhibit a knob-like protrusion, the actual purpose of which has yet to be understood. This feature is found in similar polygonal wall construction around the world. When the Spanish arrived in Peru and questioned the indigenous people there about the megalithic structures, they were told that the structures already existed when their ancestors moved into the area.

There are other physical remains that show evidence of shared knowledge around the planet. An example of this can be seen in cave construction as well. The Longyou Cave complex in China is one example of rock cutting by what appears to be a large machine. The striations left in the carved surfaces of the rocks are very similar to those found at other locations around the world. The only way similar technologies can exist in places separated by great distances and natural barriers like mountains and oceans is if someone was passing knowledge down to the people on a planetwide basis. More importantly, no one on the planet today has positively proven how these megalithic structures were created or constructed. More strangely, where are the tools and machines that enabled these grand feats? How is it possible that such knowledge has been lost? The only answer to these questions that makes sense to me is time— lots of time and possibly a near extinction-level event for humanity.

Sacsayhuaman Wall, Peru *Latina, Italy Wall* *Nimrod Castle, Israel*

There are so many clues for the existence of an earlier civilization, it is difficult to comprehend why this subject is news at all. It should be something everyone is already familiar with. How have we missed these things hiding in plain sight? Before I move on, I would like to share a couple more discoveries that support this reality. This, by the way, is not any discovery of mine. I was just as ignorant as everyone else until I learned of these things. There appears to be some type of connection between the builders of Gobekli Tepe, in Turkey, and the ancient aboriginals of Easter Island and possibly Australia as well.

T-Pillar Arm   **Urfa Man**

Note the human characteristics of this T-shaped pillar at Gobekli Tepe. The view you see represents a side view, clearly showing the arms draping down with the hands out of view as the arms wrap around the body. The hands are resting over the navel or slightly lower. This pose is mirrored in the Urfa Man statue from southeast Turkey. There are two things to note about the Urfa Man statue: the position of the hands and the appearance of a double collar on the cloak that is being worn. Now, if we look at the Moai on Easter Island in the middle of the Pacific Ocean, we see another example of this pose with the arms draped and the hands resting over the navel or slightly lower. Is this just a coincidence? I think not. Close examination of the hands reveals almost identical technical details in how the fingers are presented. I noticed immediately in both examples that no attempt was made to distinguish a thumb from any other finger. I feel this is a bit too much to be a mere coincidence. Also, why provide such a level of detail everywhere else, but totally ignore the fact that a thumb is much shorter than the other fingers? Is it even remotely possible that these figures are not human? Please don't take my word for it. Do some research and see if you agree with me or not.

Moai of Easter Island

The connection with Australia is not as strong and is not related to body parts but rather to a common word or symbol. It may be both a word and a symbol. The point is that similar symbols are found at Gobekli Tepe and in aboriginal art in Australia. A photo taken in the early 1900s of a medicine man in Australia clearly shows a three-part symbol painted on his chest and abdomen. What appears to be a similar symbol appears on one of the Gobekli Tepe pillars. One is from the twentieth century, and the other is about twelve thousand years old. I can't rule it out, but I doubt that there is actually a connection there. First, I do not see that particular symbol elsewhere in aboriginal art in Australia, and second, I believe this symbol, as presented on the Gobekli Tepe pillar, represents the expression of a meeting or a meeting place. This is completely out of context when appearing on a person's body. Once again, I must stress that this is just my opinion.

I believe that eventually, every science discipline will come to the same conclusions as I have by correlating data with what the geologists already know. It is no secret that our planet has gone through many disruptive cycles in the three or four million years that our ancestors have lived and walked upright. I consider our present human timeline to be the latest in a series of timelines going back many millions of years. It is not impossible for earlier civilizations to have existed. Perhaps we were once far more sophisticated and intelligent in the very distant past, but a catastrophe reduced our population size to almost zero. Before this, we might have had everything going for us and found life easy with amazing technology in hand. Maybe we were much larger creatures and had no trouble building megalithic structures. Then something happened that obliterated almost everything on the surface of the planet, and the few remaining humans managed to begin again as hunter-gatherers because the climate would not permit agriculture immediately after the event. As I mentioned earlier, as the ice continues to melt, I expect more spectacular finds to come to light that have been hidden for so long that they have been forgotten by humans completely. I also believe more attention needs to be focused on undersea structures, especially along the world's coastlines.

We have been lazy and have wronged ourselves and our children by accepting as truth everything we have been force-fed by our so-called leaders in education and religion. I am sure the correct thing to do today is to demand that our children be taught truth and fact. It is extremely important that every parent question what those in charge are teaching their young children, because children will believe everything you tell them until they learn to think critically. We all must stop being lazy followers like little sheep in a pasture. We must all stop behaving like a school of fish, instantly changing direction with everyone around us. We must get more involved with what our schools are doing. The sooner these discoveries are revealed to our children, the sooner they can question everything they learn about, and that is the beginning of critical thinking. It may just save our species.

CHAPTER

There's More to Us!

We have sophisticated communications systems and computers, even in poor societies. What more could we ask for? As I grow older, I find myself less in need of the trappings of society. I am more content with a few close, honest friends than most people who have hundreds of so-called online or social media friends. I have had a lot of experiences in life, and I have picked up a lot of information along the way. What took me years to learn can now be accessed immediately by anyone with a computer or a smart phone. That is great, but it looks like no one is interested in learning anything anymore. Far too many children and adults would rather play games on their technologically advanced devices than to better themselves with a little educational improvement. They are certain that there will always be someone around to provide for them when they need something. In contrast, there were people living over five thousand years ago who were highly skilled in math and science, and they knew how to survive in harsh environments. How do I know this? Well, the Giza plateau in Egypt has been giving up its secrets for hundreds of years. Not everyone was paying attention, however, until a few brilliant minds and some chance observations brought to light some absolutely amazing discoveries that have been hiding in plain sight. When or how the pyramids on the Giza plateau were actually built is not the story here;

what matters is the amount of advanced knowledge of math and astronomy that went into the design of the Giza plateau itself.

The first discovery I want to mention is not really all that important to us today, I think. It is interesting to note, however, that it has gone unnoticed for thousands of years. Keep in mind that there are absolutely no records in ancient history detailing who built the pyramids on the Giza plateau or when. Interestingly, for all of that time, everyone was certain that the pyramids were four-sided structures. Wrong! The largest of them, now known as the pyramid of Khufu, is actually an eight-sided pyramid. If you don't believe me, just Google it. In 1940, a British air force pilot flew over the great pyramid at just the right time of day to see the split shadows on one side of the structure. Pilot P. Groves photographed the pyramid that day, and the photo still amazes many people today. Most visitors will never see anything but four sides unless they take a balloon ride at just the right time of day. That is certainly an interesting fact and a wakeup call to tell us we really don't know as much as we think we do. As the photo taken by Groves shows, each face or side is really split into two different planar surfaces, divided by a vertical seam running from the apex to the base. Take a minute or two and look at the photo for yourself. My biggest question concerning this fact is about why no one— and I mean no one— knew of this until modern times. Even Egyptian historians and archaeologists were completely in the dark. This may actually support the theory that the pyramids are much more ancient than what modern scholars believe. I can only imagine what else everyone is in the dark about concerning our ancient past.

There is always another secret hiding just beyond the horizon of our present knowledge. The next discovery I would like to mention is far more complex, and some people will never accept the facts as they are now being presented by many scholars and researchers. It seems that some humans were much more educated than we believed possible five thousand years ago. Either that or we were being educated by the remnants of an earlier civilization that had existed previously on our planet— or elsewhere. It appears that the architects of the pyramids were more than mere stone masons, and it is not just what they did with any particular pyramid that amazes me. The most astonishing revelation is what they did with the three main pyramids on the Giza plateau. As I have mentioned, keep in mind that we have no way of knowing who built the pyramids and because nothing from ancient Egypt even mentions their construction, it is highly likely that they were constructed much earlier in time. That, combined with what I am about to share with you, makes the following discovery seems almost unimaginable. Actually, the facts of this discovery almost prove without a doubt that at some point, either we were visited by space travelers, or we really did have a previous civilization on our planet.

You may not believe it, but there is more to the pyramid of Khufu than just what you see on the outside or on the inside, or in the tunnels beneath the structure. It's all about the specific dimensions of the pyramid itself. One could say that Earth's major parameters are encoded in the physical dimensions of the structure. I will expand on that a little. The values for the length of the sides and the height of the pyramid are not random but carefully scaled to be related to the Earth's circumference and diameter. They had a very specific purpose for the specs they chose for the dimensions of the Great Pyramid. It does not end there! It appears that this pyramid encodes the values of Pi, Phi (the golden ratio), and E (Euler's number), which are all very important engineering constructs in use today. For me, however, the proof in the pudding is how the whole Giza plateau is laid out. The three main pyramids on the plateau are not lined up in a straight row. They are spaced apart and positioned so precisely that, if you take a photo of them from an aircraft or view them in a satellite photo, you may recognize a pattern that you have seen before. If a photo of the constellation Orion is scaled to the same physical size as a photo of the Giza plateau, you can overlay the two photos and recognize that the layout of the pyramids at Giza reflects the positions of the stars in Orion's Belt.

It gets even deeper. Some will argue that it would be necessary to flip one of the images to get them to align. That might have been the case if the Egyptians used north as "up" on their maps, but they didn't. They used south as "up," likely because from the depths of antiquity, they reasoned that water flows from top to bottom, which is south to north in their world. Exactly— the Nile River flows from south to north! In fact, if a photo of Orion is taken from a dark sky location, you will see that the pyramids, situated adjacent to the Nile River, are mirrored with the three stars of Orion's Belt, and the Milky Way appears as a river running through the center of the cosmos. Wow, wow, and holy cow! So much knowledge coming together at that one place is just amazing to me. There are other amazing facts about the Giza plateau that you should look into, such as where it is situated on the planet and the amazing coincidence about its coordinates and the speed of light. There are probably other amazing facts that we just haven't opened our eyes to yet. Please read up on some of the things mentioned here.

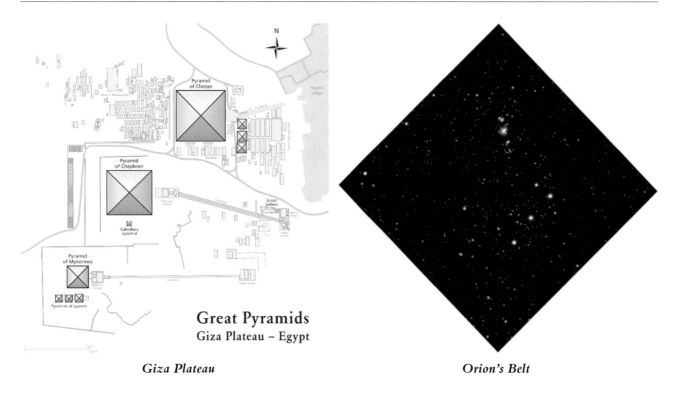

Great Pyramids
Giza Plateau – Egypt

Giza Plateau   *Orion's Belt*

Knowing about our ancient human abilities and achievements leaves me to believe that there actually was a civilization long, long ago that was planet-wide. Not only that, but they must have been in communication with everyone else, because universal myths and megastructures exist around the world. I sense that there is more to us than we ourselves realize. I am certain that we all have a little bit of our Creator in us. It seems to me that we should be capable of much, much more as a species, given what we have achieved in the past. If there really was a previous civilization, the absence of physical evidence, with the exception of the megalithic structures, leaves me to conclude that there must have been a horrific worldwide cataclysm that caused humankind to be literally wiped from the surface of the planet. The cities and communities that were present have also vanished, indicating that a tremendous amount of time has passed and that modern people are really very recent with respect to those earlier people. Without any known method to date the many megaliths around the world, we may never know just how old those earlier civilizations were. On the other hand, perhaps all that matters is that we know who we are today and, in part, how we got here. If we agree with the DNA timeline, then we really were here for millions of years, but that leaves us with the curious fact that we suddenly began to build cities and work with copper, iron, and gold just after the Younger Dryas. A sudden warming of the climate alone was just not enough of a stimulus, in my opinion.

We have to remember how we were using only tools and weapons made from stone for millions of years prior to the Younger Dryas period. It is obvious something occurred that directly affected humanity almost overnight, historically speaking. I know I may change my mind someday when more information becomes available, but I honestly believe that we, Homo sapiens, were modified in some way that resulted in our immediate success as a species. I am starting to take seriously those cuneiform writings that tell of the modification or creation of people by God-like beings. No one today can say exactly what is real and what is fiction in these writings, but someone thought it important enough to document these stories thousands of years ago. Why would they do that? My take is simply because they could! With limited resources at hand, our ancestors were clever enough to ensure that their knowledge would last forever. I believe they lost it once and were very much afraid of losing it again. Somehow, someway, survivors of a great calamity had lost all their prior knowledge and had to start over. That was reason enough to want to remember and preserve past knowledge.

Aside from our knowledge of math, engineering, medicine, and other physical sciences, there may be another dimension to our existence. Humans have been experimenting with other aspects of our existence for hundreds, if not thousands of years. Altered states of consciousness are not something that just started back in the '60s during the hippie movement. Most people don't even realize that recreational drugs have been around for a very long time. In the past, mind-altering drugs were even used in religious ceremonies. They were in many places around the planet in ages past, but it is highly likely that the public did not have the access or knowledge to utilize them in ancient times. As to be expected, they were used for medicinal purposes as well. Today, there are many artificially manufactured drugs in communities around the world. Simply put, it is big business. The gods gave us free will, and if we are stupid enough to get involved with street drugs, the dealers are more than willing to take our money, even if we may die as a result. It is simply not their problem; it's just business!

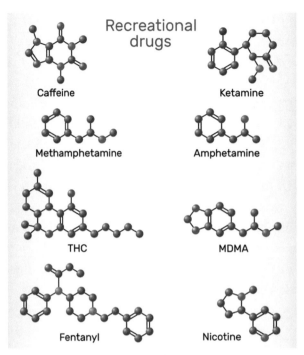

Recreational Drugs

There are, of course, many prescription drugs that are very dangerous as well. We must never take for granted that, just because a professional has prescribed a medication for us, it is not without risks. Think critically and always learn as much as you can about the medications you are prescribed. Sounds like common sense to me, but I know many people who never question their doctors about anything. Doctors have been using all kinds of drugs to treat people's various complaints, from headaches to hypertension, but did you know many of the so-called recreational drugs can be found on the shelf at pharmacies around the world? Cocaine, at one time, was the worst drug on the street, but many doctors prescribed it regularly. Believe it or not, up until the early twentieth century, cocaine was legal for general consumption. In fact, it was one of the main two ingredients in Coca-Cola. It's true, cocaine and caffeine, hence the name, were the two main ingredients. It was originally formulated as a patent medicine around 1888, but later, around the turn of the century, public pressure succeeded in having the drink modified and the cocaine completely removed from its recipe.

There is another history lesson there, but I will leave it for you to discover on your own. I mentioned earlier that drugs like cocaine were in use in ancient times. As it so happens, so was marijuana. In 2020, a researcher discovered an alter in the Negev desert that contained ashes that were preserved by the ultra-dry climate. The Jewish temple dates back to around 500 BCE, and a careful examination of these ashes revealed traces of tetrahydrocannabinol (THC), the active ingredient in marijuana. It was a curious find considering that the Torah makes no mention at all about this plant. It is a known fact, however, that not only were the leaves of the marijuana plant used by the ancients, but the hemp fiber of its sister plant, Cannabis sativa L, was utilized in different ways based on availability and need. To this day, clothing is manufactured in some parts of the world from hemp fibers. A hemp rope can be used to break down huge rocks into more manageable pieces. It seems that if you pull a rope of hemp tightly into a crack in a rock and then apply water, the hemp expands slowly, but with great force. If properly tensioned, the expansion can break the crack open. Now, that is not something you would expect to see every day, so where did they get that knowledge from? The Egyptians were brilliant in being able to utilize the natural resources they had at their disposal. During my research, I also learned that scientific analysis of the remains of some Egyptian mummies revealed that their body tissue contained traces of THC and cocaine. I couldn't help but wonder if this was the result of medicinal treatment or just plain privilege.

Some two thousand years before the time of the temple ashes that I mentioned earlier, cannabis was apparently in use in China. Hollowed-out wooden burners were found at a cemetery in the Pamir mountains with high concentrations of THC in the ashes. Being found at a cemetery indicates that their presence was likely related to religious practices and not recreational use. Other ancient cemeteries farther north in China, as well as some in the Altai Mountains of Russia, indicate that this was common practice over great distances. Research further reveals that the hemp plant has been in cultivation for over four thousand years. The question is, of course, why were people everywhere getting high on mind-altering drugs? Is there something about our minds that we just do not have knowledge of in the modern era?

I have heard many people say that mind-altering substances like LSD, magic mushrooms, peyote, and PCP all enable you to allow your mind to transcend your body and travel to other places and times. I think that is a bit of nonsense, even if I will never know for sure because I will never expose myself to such drugs. I won't rule out, however, that while a person's mind is in an altered state, it may be in the condition necessary for us to connect with a universal force or energy. I am thinking, perhaps, it is like the process of tuning your radio dial to the station you want to listen to. An altered mental state may relieve the mind of the workload required to handle millions of signals every second as our brains process all of the data coming in from our senses. The mind can then utilize all of its power to concentrate on a single frequency that connects all things, if that is possible.

I know it all sounds kind of silly, but as with everything else I have mentioned, I have a reason for discussing it. We really are more than we realize, and we really can do things most people would simply refute outright. Pretty much everyone on the planet is familiar with terms like *medicine man*, *sangoma*, or *shaman*. They all serve important functions in their communities, such as passing on oral traditions and histories, as well as healing the sick and injured. They are also tasked with educating their communities and training the next shaman down the line. It isn't what they do that is so fascinating but rather their way of doing it. Modern society relies almost completely on modern hospitals, clinics, and doctor's offices to deal with matters of health. In places like central Australia, Amazonia, and even the cold climates of Canada and Siberia, aboriginal shaman are the local doctors of their isolated communities. Shamanism appears to be waning in modern times, but it is what was happening in past that I am interested in. It seems that the ancient shamans were able to affect change simply by speaking or chanting while in an altered state of mind.

Is this a lost art? More and more research is revealing that we can actually heal ourselves by creating the right environment for our brains and by concentrating on the healing process. Some people use the phrase "getting in touch with the cosmos" to refer to receiving healing energy directly from the universe. Others say that a shaman can channel that energy to heal the sick or bring about physical changes in a person, such as changes in attitude or temperament. Is this what priests do during an exorcism? I must admit my skepticism, but at the same time, I have been told that I have a very warm and calming touch. Perhaps we were once able to channel energy for various reasons, and maybe some people still can. Are the names Edgar Cayce and Nostradamus familiar to you? Edgar Cayce seems to have been able to see into the future, and Nostradamus seems to have had success with healing. Could they have been shaman and just did not realize it during their lives?

We really don't know ourselves as much as we think we do. We still can't figure out how to fix mental illnesses or stop crimes or take care of the homeless. Only recently have we begun to understand that nothing is black and white. Even autism occurs as a spectrum of symptoms, and yet, we tend to concentrate on the symptoms instead of the person. I am not a doctor and I have little experience with autism, but of this much, I am sure: what you see is just the cover of the book, and there could be a genius hiding inside an autistic person that just needs some help escaping. The truth is, we all may suffer from some degree of autism or other so-called mental illness. Perhaps we all should just stop throwing stones! Being different does not mean that a person is somehow not normal. In fact, that word, *normal*, just happens to be the most misused word in the English language, in my opinion. So-called normal behavior is a completely subjective concept on par with words like *"pornography"* and *"etiquette"*. Everyone has his or her own opinion on where to draw the line, or he or she has his or her own definition for these concepts. One person's artistic expression is another person's profanity. My point for this discussion is that we must all be truthful with ourselves and try to understand why we think the way we do about various concepts. We must recognize our acquired paradigms and learn to examine our feelings. We really can change and shed some of the old baggage that has been heaped upon us through the years. Do we think a certain way about a particular subject because we believe in a principle, or do we think that way because someone else told us that is how we should think? Think about it! Are you your own person or does someone else pull your strings? I believe we all have it in us to lead our own lives and to become more than what we are today. We just have to stop playing follow the leader, especially when we are not the leader.

On another side note, I would like to challenge every single reader of this book to take the time to look at a YouTube clip of an episode of *AGT* (*America's Got Talent*) from May of 2019, starring a young singer named Codi Lee. Try to find the longer clip of his first audition that includes his introduction with his mother and a short backstory. This video clip made me think a little differently about autism and about how we perceive things in general. Another video clip that may surprise you and also emphasizes that we should never assume anything, is the first appearance of Susan Boyle on *BGT* (*Britain's Got Talent*) in May of 2019. You may be able to find these two videos just by using the Google search function on your browser. This is who we are today. We are not one of anything. We are everything, and it is up to us all to make the most of all that we have and be our best at whatever we do in life.

CHAPTER

Critical Thinking—Can it Help?

We have been lazy and have wronged ourselves and our children by accepting as truth everything we have been force-fed by our so-called leaders in education and religion. As I have previously mentioned, I am sure the correct thing to do today is to demand that our children be taught truth and fact. It is extremely important that every parent questions what people are teaching young children because children will believe everything you tell them until they learn to think critically. We must stop being lazy followers like little sheep in a pasture. We must all stop behaving like a school of fish that instantly changes direction with the rest of the school. We must get more involved with what our educators are doing. The sooner these discoveries are revealed to our children, the sooner they can question everything they learn, and that is the beginning of critical thinking. It may just save our species.

You may think I am just trying to lecture people about raising their children in this chapter, but if you read this with an open mind and keep it in context with the rest of this book, you will understand both the reason I write about it here and its relevance to the overall subject matter. I feel compelled to express my thoughts on this subject because it really is pertinent to our very future. I would like to think that our schools are teaching our children how to lead instead of follow. Sounds simple, and you might take it for granted. It is great for our children to learn about the past, but that does not mean they have to think the way people did in the past. Training in critical thinking can begin at almost any age, and the sooner the better.

I know that, as a parent, raising children is not an easy task. What parents underestimate is the need to be communicative with their children. One of the most frequent questions children have is, "Why?" Answering with "because I said so" is a huge mistake. Many parents fail here because they simply do not understand how important it is for a child to have a reason for everything. I understand that most parents get very tired of hearing question after question and that sometimes they are just plain tired. If only you could feel the frustration your children feel when they are dismissed from their questions with answers that make absolutely no sense to them. It really would be better if you were absolutely honest with them. If you don't know something, simply say so. Your child will still love you. But by all means, take that as a challenge to find out the correct answer to their questions and, if it gets to be too much, just call for a time-out. You would be surprised to learn how much children really understand. Just don't brush them off because that hurts. Also, make it clear to your child whether or not your answer is believed to be a fact or just an opinion. The sooner he or she can separate fact from opinion, the sooner the child will learn to think critically. Please, for the sake of humanity, do not raise your children to be followers! The gods of antiquity that made us in their image were leaders in society as should our children be.

Humankind's Best Resource

So, how do we tell if what we are being told is fact, opinion, or just plain fiction? First, to find the truth, you must be willing to seek the truth. By that, I mean you should read this material with an open mind and be as critical as you can be, using what you already know, not what you already believe.

Remember, if you are more than three years old, you are already brainwashed and have been continually acquiring paradigms. The facts and opinions I propose are not an end point, but quite to the contrary: they are a starting point. Keep in mind that I am not a biblical scholar or anything else other than a person with a strong desire to find the truth in all things. If you want to know who and what you are, look inside. Stand in front of a mirror if you have to, and face yourself. Do you believe you can really know more about yourself today than you did yesterday? I believe you can! Try this type of exercise to distract your mind from the stresses of the moment. Simple thoughts seem to work more effectively. Invent your own distraction techniques. It also helps if you don't drink any caffeine beverages near bedtime. Counting sheep is an old-fashioned method and may work for some people, but there are also other methods to calm the mind. Try paying special attention to your breathing when you first lie down to sleep. Try to deliberately slow down your rate of breathing until you start to relax, which should take only a minute or two. I find that if I take in a little extra air and hold it in my lungs for a few extra seconds, my heart rate begins to drop and I begin to relax. Then I breathe normally and stay as relaxed as possible. I also have a favorite CD with piano lullaby music that helps me relax and fall into a sound sleep. It usually works within ten minutes. Some folks just leave the TV on and fall asleep listening to the news or other useless noise.

I want to give you one more example of what I believe will help you get to know yourself a little better. This exercise has never failed to help me not only fall asleep more quickly but also help in other ways as well. When you lie down to sleep, think of some unresolved problem that you would like to see get resolved. I enjoy the study of subatomic particles, especially photons because they are so difficult to describe. Ask any physicist what a single photon is, and his or her answer may surprise you. He or she might even say, "I haven't a clue." When I lie down to sleep, I place myself in research mode. I review in my mind everything that I have already learned about the subject matter and try to understand more deeply the intricacies involved and how I might think about it differently. I do some "if-then" exercises in my mind to come up with a way to prove one theory or another. I know you are not interested in such silliness, but surely there is something in your life that needs this type of contemplation. It could be a problem at work or school, or maybe a plan you may want to put into motion in the near future like a trip overseas, buying a beach house, building a workshop, or something else.

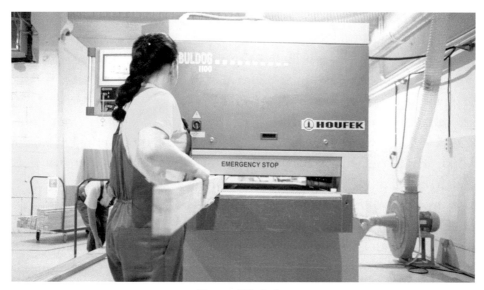

Dream Workshop

The subject matter in our lives is of little importance; the process is everything! Many people do not realize that when you sleep, your brain does not slow down. Because it is relieved of the workload that is required to assist you with your awake functions, it now has excess computational power to help you with logical problems. Many people swear that things they have had on their minds always seem clearer after a good night's sleep. Now you know why. Even if a problem is complex, concentrating on only one thing is the key to how this works. So, how does this help you get to know yourself better? If you use this technique often, you will start to become more aware of yourself both physically and mentally. The very first time you find yourself asking why you feel a certain way about something, especially if it is a new feeling or sensation, that is your mind getting in tune with your body and then a process of self-examination evolves, sometimes completely subconsciously. You are critically thinking about not only some subject matter, but self as well. You do not have to take my word for it, but at least give it a try. It couldn't hurt and might, if nothing else, help you to get a good night's sleep. It might even give you more insight and confidence about yourself and those around you. Do not be afraid to ask yourself or your friends difficult questions. The only bad question is the question not asked! Don't be afraid to question an answer you've been given if it is not completely clear or meaningful to you. Again I remind you: only you can prevent ignorance in your life.

If you decide to research some of the subject matter I have covered— and I hope you do— enjoy the learning process. Seek out others who may have a similar interest. Share your newfound knowledge with family and friends. You will find yourself living a more fulfilling life. You may even start a snowball event. Imagine a snowball rolling downhill. It starts out about the size of your fist and then quickly grows in size as it picks up more and more snow along its path. You are the snowball, and as you share your knowledge with others and they each share their knowledge with others, eventually the knowledge becomes widespread and ignorance is diminished. This is especially true if the knowledge was obtained through a process of critical thinking, making it much more likely to be accurate and true in nature. We can all make a difference in this world, and this is one of the easiest ways to do just that.

Humanity has almost forgotten the importance of conversation and debate. For this reason especially, we need to ensure that our children are being taught not only about how to be leaders but also about how to use critical thinking to find their way through so much media crap and misinformation. As for personal experiences, I have seen within my own circle of family members and friends how uniformed many people are. From simple, everyday merchandising tricks to political misinformation, many people are inclined to be lazy about trying to get to the truth. A good simple example I see all the time is the "BOGO" offers. BOGO stands for buy one, get one, usually at a discounted price or even for free. The lazy -minded folks snap up what they believe to be a bargain and haven't a clue that the other stores a few blocks away have a better price for the same product. If you see an item priced at three for twelve dollars at one store but "buy two, get one free" at another store, which is the better deal? A lazy mind will simply go for the get-one-free trap. A critical thinker will immediately want to know the price of a single unit of the product at the store with the BOGO sale. If the unit price is not displayed, then it is likely going to cost you more to buy the product at that store. If that product costs you seven dollars each at the BOGO store and you have to pay for only two of them, that is still fourteen dollars for three of them. You spent two dollars more than you needed to for the same product elsewhere.

BOGO *Sale*

This is just one of many simple merchandising tricks that businesses know they can get away with just because people are lazy-minded and will not put the effort into thinking critically. Another simple trick is to raise the price of an item so much that a store can offer it for sale at, say, 40 percent off and still make more profit than if they just sold it at its presale price. Most people cannot afford to be tricked in this way, as their incomes are barely above the poverty level, if not below. As it turns out, these are the folks most likely to be without a clue and who have no critical-thinking skills. Why? Well, because they simply cannot afford the education that others can. How can a person pay for or find the time for a better education when he or she is working two jobs? Big businesses know this, but they just don't give a damn. They want to make a profit, and they are more than happy to take advantage of our ignorance.

The bottom line is that I do believe a society with strong critical-thinking skills will be more likely to see the truth in everything, from politics to religion and even to simple merchandising. In general, more educated people are less likely to be followers and are more inclined to make their own decisions.

I know there are exceptions, especially for those folks that have extreme tendencies, that is to say, those with a closed mind. Yes, we must also ensure that our schools are promoting open-mindedness and kindness toward all people. Nature makes us what we are, and not one of us is above another. I reiterate: we desperately need to teach our children these skills. I know this section sounds entirely off topic, but do not forget how we came to be who and what we are.

We have been given great abilities that allow us to control our destinies, but we must pass that knowledge onto our children or we will end up being nothing more than sheep again. If a school or school system is not teaching children at a level equal to or above the level of the rest of your nation's schools, then your government must step in and determine why this is the case. The failing schools need to be shut down, and your children need to be given every opportunity to be educated on par with all the other children in the country. No more dumbing down schools to make the school systems feel better. That is not what education should be about. A whole lot more of the national budget needs to be spent on school systems and teachers to ward off dumbing down society in the coming generations. The truth is that our education problems are easy to fix. Two major areas need to be addressed to set up an education system that will work for a change anywhere in the world. One is, of course, the funding I mentioned already. The second is the most important of all. One word: *accountability*!

Students and their parents must learn, starting at the preschool level, that rules apply to everyone. The parents must be held accountable for the actions and behaviors of their children all through their school years. That includes any foster or adopted parents or other family members the children live with. Any child who interferes with the ability of other children to learn must be critiqued and, if necessary, removed from that environment. The outcomes can be quite varied, from insertion into special schools or possibly into a trade school, if appropriate. It is well known, though quite often ignored, that many children do not do well in a standard classroom environment. The reasons are many, but that in no way points to any fault on the child's part. Each child is an individual and must be treated as such. We cannot go on treating our school children like cattle or sheep, expecting them all to behave and to respond in the same manner. I can still remember the pain of a heavy ruler across my knuckles because I could not write with my right hand. Being left-handed in a right-handed world has always been an issue, but the worst was when I was in grade school. Because of the way I was treated, I actually believed I was doing something wrong. Of course, it couldn't have been the nuns doing something wrong! In any case, I hope the nuns of today are more educated, more compassionate, and willing to think more critically.

Wouldn't it be great if all educators were experts in the subjects they teach? If the technical colleges and universities need more teachers in specific areas such as computer-related courses or materials science or engineering, then it should be a simple matter of hiring the right people. The financial incentives for hiring retired workers from these fields must be provided to the schools. There are certainly plenty of candidates available, if only they would be offered a realistic salary that would make it worth their time and effort. The simple truth is, we do not have a lack of teachers around the world; what we have is a lack of interest in funding them to do the most important job in the world: to pass on knowledge. My simple mind tells me that critical thinking can and does help one to find the truth, and that is what this entire book is about. Think critically and find the truth in every aspect of your life. Be happy that you have a wonderful mind and move with confidence throughout your journey.

Tech School Student

Knowledge can take you to places you have yet to imagine. You probably figured out by now that I am a proponent of education. I am, but I believe that every nation on the planet needs to look carefully at what is being prioritized in every curriculum. Are we going to continue teaching every student to be a copy of every other student? Are we unconsciously trying to eliminate natural diversity in our children? To what end? Maybe we think it is a more efficient way to educate the masses. Sorry, but I don't agree with the argument that the children of the world are just part of some mass that requires education! With that attitude, all we have is a society without any texture and simply an amorphous mass that has the property that no single unit is recognizable. Perhaps the whole world needs to rethink education. I believe that a major function of any educational system is to examine students individually to determine their strong points and to foster their interests to improve their successes in adulthood. Only then should students be placed in classes with others requiring the same subject matter.

I honestly believe that not nearly enough emphasis is placed on this manner of education. After all, knowledge and commitment may be needed to keep us from annihilation when Earth experiences the next major catastrophe. Wait, what catastrophe? Well, some say it is just a matter of time. Remember, the Earth has seen numerous catastrophes in the past, some minor and some major. Some of the worst catastrophes on Earth were actually the result of a visitor from space. It seems that when the Earth is devastated by an asteroid strike, a series of events unfolds that is much more destructive than the initial impact. Considering our level of readiness (not!), I fear the next major event will end humanity. Our story doesn't have to end that way if we don't want it to. May the force be with us!

CHAPTER

The Next Catastrophe— Will We Survive?

Consider what would happen if a global catastrophe occurred tomorrow. A large asteroid could easily wipe out 95 percent or more of the population on the planet. The more dependent we become on technology, the less likely we are to survive intact as a species, should a serious catastrophe occur. Countries like Canada, the United States, England, Italy, France, Spain, Germany, and more would likely suffer most. Smaller, island nations would simply disappear under the waves. The urban areas in countries like China and Russia would also be lost simply because of the population density. The only real chance of surviving an event that affects the whole planet would rest with the people who are more self-sufficient and who have a great deal of knowledge about self-reliance and sustainability. Think in terms of the people who lived seven thousand to twelve thousand years ago. A major catastrophe would shut down most, if not all, of our technology in a matter of days or even hours. A nuclear winter would set in that could last for decades or even centuries. We would not have enough time to tool up and create alternate living conditions that would be required for us and for the animal population to survive. Maybe that is what we should be thinking about instead of waging war on each other, both on the national level and the personal level.

I challenge the younger generation to think about these things and to change the political landscape. I challenge our present leaders worldwide to begin building the necessary underground infrastructure for producing energy, creating farming structures, manufacturing facilities, and other facilities that any civilization would need to survive. We may find that we won't have to live off world after all. Colonizing a distant planet gives us no guarantee that an asteroid won't strike there. I know it is a scary thought and that many readers will think I may be sensationalizing with these kinds of foreboding ramblings. That, however, is far from the truth. Everyone in the world with any interest in astronomy already knows that it is just a matter of time before the Earth and a significant asteroid end up in the same place at the same time. We already know what the end result will be as well. We have only one way to avoid extinction, and that is to go underground. Can we start planning that today, please? The gods have blessed us with a marvelous powerful brain, so let's begin to use it.

Scientists have proven beyond a doubt that small- to medium-sized space rocks can have their trajectories altered by crashing into them with a human-made craft or by pushing them into an altered orbit if we detect one headed our way. The problem is, we must first be aware of its presence, and we must be able to study it's orbital parameters for a long enough period to know how to intervene. Additionally, we may not be able to do anything to effectively alter an extremely large asteroid simply because it is much too massive. Our best bet would be to go underground for as long as necessary to avoid a total reset of our species. Believe it or not, we already have the knowledge and the technology to do this. All we are lacking is the willpower.

If you want some simple inspiration, just look at Google Maps and search for Arizona Crater, also known as the Barringer Crater. A solid, iron-and-nickel space rock traveling at about 26,000 MPH blasted a hole in the ground over 550 feet deep, leaving a crater that measures almost three-quarters of a mile wide. This event happened about fifty thousand years ago. Can you imagine the aftermath if another event like this one occurred in some populated area of the world today? The Barringer Crater, by the way, is quite small when compared with many of the other craters discovered around the globe. Take some time off from watching sitcoms and check out this subject matter for yourself. Most importantly, find some YouTube videos of the meteorite that landed in Chelyabinsk, Russia, in 2013. The shock waves from this event injured more than a thousand people, and the videos are a must-see for educational purposes.

Barringer Crater—Arizona, USA

Bolide

Also, humans have used caves, both natural and human-made, to avoid turmoil on the surface in the past. Primitive, natural cave dwellings are being found on a regular basis. Occasionally, human-made caves are discovered as well. Some of them are quite large and can house many thousands of people. The Derinkuyu cave system in Turkey is an astounding example of a human-made cave system that was capable of supporting an estimated twenty thousand people. It is constructed with eighteen levels below ground and is complete with ventilation shafts, wells, and storage areas. Also found therein are kitchens, school rooms, wineries, and living spaces, as well as a bathhouse. Considering that this cave system is nearly three thousand years old, I would think we could build some similar underground structures today that could be used for designated purposes. Everything we do now as a society, from farming to manufacturing, could theoretically be done in a well-engineered cave system.

Underground City in Turkey

If we can figure out how to survive on Mars, then we certainly should be able to figure out how to survive on our home planet! Fifty years ago, this would have been considered science fiction, but today we really do have the technology and knowledge to pull this off. The biggest problem we face is laziness and inaction. For all our blessings of having been given great minds and imaginations, it is our lazy nature that may ensure our demise. That is a sad thought, indeed. It really doesn't have to end up that way. We can write a happy ending to this chapter if our leaders are willing to be the leaders they were elected to be. As tax-paying individuals, we deserve a voice, and we must use it to direct our leaders down the necessary paths to get this ball rolling before it is too late. If our leaders are not willing to help humanity protect itself, then it is time to change the leadership using any legal means at our disposal, starting with the vote. If we find ourselves in line for an asteroid strike, there won't be any prayer that can help, only an intelligent response by humanity to protect itself so that we may rise again.

Remember, nature has already been set in motion, and we cannot change the course of events relating to natural phenomena. We know from geological records that volcanoes, earthquakes, impacts, and ice ages have occurred in the past at mostly irregular intervals and that there is no reason to believe these won't continue. Shall we sit and cry like a baby when disaster strikes, or shall we begin our effort to mitigate the impact of such a future disaster? If you read this, please reach out to your leadership and demand help with this looming human problem. We have no idea when a major problem will arise, but we are certain that it will happen eventually. We have close calls several times a year where an unseen asteroid goes zipping by perilously close to our planet. These are usually smaller space rocks anywhere from the size of a small car to several meters in diameter. That is why they are unseen, sometimes until after they pass. A real threat exists from any asteroids coming from the direction of the sun because they are much harder to see, even if they are large. Even if we knew where every asteroid was located today, we still could not predict exactly where they might be in a few years. A passing object from outside of our solar system or a new object dislodged from the asteroid belt or another unknown location can interact with any of the many thousands of asteroids lurking within reach of our planet.

Danger can be found in almost any sized meteoroid that comes our way. Smaller space objects enter our atmosphere all the time. Many remain unseen because they burn up over remote areas or over the vast oceans around the planet. More and more are being recorded, however, because of the rapid increase in the use of dash cams and security cameras. These meteors flash brightly and usually last for a few seconds or less. Occasionally, a very large object creates a momentary fireball that is sometimes brighter than daylight as it burns and explodes in the atmosphere. These are called bolides, and the pieces that survive and crash on the surface of our planet are called meteorites. A recent traumatic event occurred in the city of Chelyabinsk in Siberia in 2013. Please check out the YouTube videos of this event that injured approximately a thousand people when the shock wave from the exploding bolide caught the population off guard. The blast from the air explosion blew out windows for miles around and even knocked down the wall of a building and blew doors off their hinges. Most injuries, as you might have guessed, were caused by flying glass. Watch these videos and learn from them. The knowledge you gain might just save your life someday.

Just for the hell of it, Google the words "Canadian meteorite" and learn how close to being hit by a space rock some people were. Or how about waking up with a meteorite in your bed just inches from your head? Yeah, it happened! Scientists are finding more evidence of impact sites in places like the recent find under the Greenland ice sheet and the Chicxulub crater in Mexico's Yucatan peninsula. At 31 km wide (19.3 miles), the Greenland crater, located under the Hiawatha glacier, was an event that could have had global impacts some fifty-eight million year ago, according to recent studies. The Chicxulub crater is about five times larger and most certainly was the result of a worldwide extinction event. Additionally, a crater discovered in Russia that appears to be from the same time period hints at the Earth having been struck by multiple bolides sixty-six million years ago. It really happens. Some would say that, statistically speaking, it is not likely for us to see another huge asteroid strike on our planet anytime in the near future. Even if that is correct, it is still just a statistical measure that in no way guarantees it won't happen next Friday— just saying!

Coming Soon to a Location Near You!

I probably would not have suggested that there is an urgency for establishing a means of surviving below the surface if it was based solely on the possibility of an asteroid strike. There are also other reasons to do so. I have always been curious about the nature of sunspots. Today, scientists tell us that sunspots are basically areas of the sun's surface that are cooler than the surrounding areas. I have heard and read various claims that try to explain in detail just what is happening there and the possible causes. Do you remember all of the hype around the comet Shoemaker-Levy 9 (SL-9) that was ripped apart by the gravity of the planet Jupiter prior to impacting that planet in 1994? It left huge scars in Jupiter's atmosphere, and when I see photos of those impacts, I immediately notice the similarities with sun spots. I could be completely off base here, but could sunspots be the results of solar impacts? In any case, the Jupiter event in 1994 was most definitely a wake-up call. The general expression *planetary defense* may have been in use prior to this event, but by 1998, a strategic planetary defense program was in place with a goal of finding 90 percent of all asteroids one kilometer or larger that are likely to cross our path. If an object the size of SL-9 impacted our sun, the disturbance to the solar atmosphere could cause an atmospheric eruption known as a solar flare. Solar flares that emit matter that reaches Earth can cause damage and even the complete loss of some of our satellites and earthbound communication systems. We should be able to survive that event without going underground, but another type of solar flare may make it prudent for us to get out of the light. That would be a supernova of a star close enough to irradiate Earth with muons and other forms of radiation for a long enough period to severely weaken or even strip away our ozone layer. Radiation from the event as well as background space radiation would reach the surface of the planet, possibly causing an extinction-level event. If nothing else, long-term exposure to high-energy radiation would endanger our existence by damaging the DNA of plant and animal life, including us. As if that is not enough to worry about, I have to mention volcanism.

In my opinion, volcanism is the most likely near-term issue that should seriously concern us with respect to moving underground, or at least moving our agricultural systems there. Except for the people living along the ring of fire, most folks have no idea what is happening in the world today with volcanism. To understand what I mean by "the ring of fire," just Google it and you will see a map of the oceans perimeters that roughly correspond to the edges of the Earth's tectonic plates. Most of the world's volcanoes are located along the boundaries where the plates meet. There are other locations, but generally those volcanoes pose a lessor threat, as I understand it. At least one mass extinction on our planet has been attributed to volcanism. It was basically a large-scale, long-term eruption from fissures in the earth that were miles long. About sixty-six thousand years ago, the ground opened in what is now known as western India and deposited layer after layer of magma over the surface to a depth of more than 2 km (1.2 mi). Geologists today refer to this structure as the Deccan Traps. Google it for more info.

One of Earth's largest extinctions, however, occurred about 250 million years ago and killed of over 90 percent of all life on the planet. This was a long-term event lasting for thousands of years. When it was over, it is estimated that 96 percent of all marine life had perished. The point is that it was a long-term event and was not likely the first one, and we now know that it wasn't the last one (remember India?). It doesn't take a lot of imagination to wonder when the next one will come. The most important takeaway from this discussion is that we do not know what initiated the eruptions in the first place. Could it have been caused by asteroid impacts? Also, how does volcanism kill ocean-dwelling lifeforms? Well, it is all about the gases that are ejected into the atmosphere. Without writing a whole chapter on biology and chemistry, let me just say that multiple gases escape into the atmosphere that can have both short-term and long-term effects on animals and vegetation. If allowed to continue over long periods of time, the effects become accumulative and work their way into environments that are not necessarily in direct contact with the volcanism. An example of this is how certain gases in the atmosphere can cause rain to become very acidic. The long-term addition of acidic rainwater over the oceans causes the sea water to become acidic. This, in turn, creates other reactions that change the water from a life-giving resource into what can be described as a dead pool, with insufficient oxygen to support life.

Please don't even think that this cannot happen in our time and therefore, there is no reason to think about it. It likely will not happen in our time, but we must think about it now. If we ignore it and it occurs, how will we cope? Should we remain unconcerned and just let our grandchildren worry about it when it happens to them? Somehow, I think this scenario also repeats itself throughout time. I am talking about people ignoring the past and learning nothing from it. Maybe it is what brought down so many civilizations in the past. I am certain you are very familiar with the expression about history repeating itself. We need to act now, while we still have access to all of our technology and resources. The things we need to accomplish may not be possible if we are suffering and fighting for resources. As I mentioned earlier, we must challenge our leaders to at least start with the planning phase for our transition to a subsurface existence. Please review and critique everything I have written and make up your own mind as to whether or not this action is prudent. If everyone knows what may lie ahead for us, then perhaps we have a chance. We certainly don't want our great-grandchildren to say that they thought we were much smarter and wonder how we could have ignored these issues instead of taking action. It would look to future generations like we were nothing more than a bunch of brain-dead gods. Well, technically speaking, maybe we really are. Let's get our brains in gear and start changing the way we do things. We must consider how we are writing the history of humanity today.

CHAPTER

Conclusion—I Know!

OK, so now we know what it means to be human. We also know from ancient stone tablets that we, as hominids, were modified in some way by ancient visitors to our planet. We were made in their image, but not necessarily in the literal sense. You decide. In any case, the evidence at hand points to the fact that we are as capable as they once were. We have the most evolved minds of any creature on the planet, and we have the gift of free will. No one can tell you what to believe. Even if you are completely against the idea that there is any truth in ancient texts and scriptures, there is still the physical evidence all over the planet that suggests we do not know much about our very distant past. As far as a choice goes between visitors to our planet versus an ancient civilization, I am leaning toward a visitation since we have no physical evidence of a previous advanced civilization. Well, we do have those megaliths everywhere, so maybe a previous civilization was destroyed and some "ET" visitors helped us to get back on track. I can't wait to hear the ending of that story. Also, we must admit to ourselves that we still believe we owe our modifiers (not the Creator) some sort of allegiance or piety. We must learn to kick that monkey off our backs. Our destiny as a species is entirely up to us. No gods are going to come help us when catastrophe strikes. The Creator has already set in motion the laws of the universe. We, here and now, are as gods upon the Earth. We are the masters and lords of this planet. I wonder if that means we are doomed!

We cannot deny our accomplishments, which are truly awesome. We analyze things on a molecular level and build huge structures and send our probes to other planets and beyond. In case you didn't already know, we have two spacecrafts that have recently traveled beyond the edges of our solar system and are now traveling through interstellar space. If only we could travel far enough back in time to witness our transformation from Stone-Age knuckle-draggers to the modern sapiens that we have become. Perhaps then we could better understand why there are so many cryptic stories carved in stone. I am referring to the stories of the gods and the demigods who walked alongside humans in ancient times. Perhaps there are no more demigods to be found on the planet in modern times. If you know anyone who is more than a couple hundred years old, that person may be a candidate. There are, however, many giants remaining. These are people of great renown who have pushed the boundaries and accomplished great things for the betterment of humanity. They may not be a hundred feet tall, but their deeds are exceedingly great. To get an idea of who these people are, just Google the Nobel Peace Prize winners. Seriously, many giants will never be heard of or mentioned in the media. They are dedicated people capable of loving and caring for others without any need for recognition or reward. Their nationalities, financial situations, or religious associations do not matter at all. They may not even realize that they require no leadership from any human institutions whatsoever. That is because they are the leaders of society themselves, doing what needs to be done to make the world thrive. It does not matter what they do for a living, either. Some of them are nurses, doctors, teachers, engineers, cooks, and tradespeople.

Lastly, there is God. If there is anything that humans seem to overlook, it is the very nature of God. As I mentioned earlier, we owe all of our piety and allegiance to the mother of all that is, Mother Nature! Our saving grace will come in the form of educating ourselves and our children and in demanding that our nations work together with a planetwide commitment to one another and to love and respect nature. At some point, we must begin to hold corporations responsible for damages they cause and demand they repair it with programs of reclamation, reforestation, and remediation. At the same time, individuals must do their part to reduce human demand for products that can only be produced by activities that are causing the damage. It is a tough nut to crack, but at the same time, I believe the key to opening that shell is education.

Are you willing to better society and make the world a more enjoyable place to live? I cannot tell you how to live your life and neither can anyone else. However, each one of us can choose to learn what can be done on an individual basis to improve our own impacts on the planet. I remember an old expression from my childhood: "Waste not, want not." Everything we do should be out of a need, not necessarily a want. Having enough money to buy anything you need is great, but buying anything you want is a serious issue for everyone. When people buy excessive amounts of food, for example, much of it is simply going to end up as waste. This logic holds true for most anything. If we produce waste for people who don't know what to do with their money, we are increasing the amount of damage we do in nature. Corporations want you to buy as much as possible, and they really don't care much about what happens to the environment as a result. We all need certain things in life if we are to remain civilized, but do we really need as much as we consume on an individual basis? Remember, less purchasing means we make a smaller footprint, which in turn means that resources last longer. A side benefit is that inflation is also kept in check as a result. It's a complicated balancing act, but that's the key. We must do our best to find balance in all areas of our lives. At the same time, we must demand openness and accountability from corporations and they must provide a means to replenish what they are taking from the Earth where practicable. The Earth is here for all humans. It does not belong only to powerful organizations or governments.

Finally, I would like to mention this while discussing our resources. I was appalled a couple of years ago when I heard about companies planning to set up mining operations on the moon. Yes, our moon. The problem with that is maybe those idiots really don't know or just don't care that the Earth and the moon operate together as a system. No moon mean no tides! Mess with the moon, and you are messing with Earth. Show me the studies that prove mining the moon will have no effect on planet Earth! I am certain that the only reason for such an undertaking is that there is a large profit to be had for someone in a position of authority. If you ever have any opportunity to weigh in on this subject matter, please make your voice heard.

So, what can we do about these questions? Three words will answer that question concisely. Seek the truth! We owe it to our children and our grandchildren and future generations. It would be better for our offspring in the distant future to be praising us for being foresighted enough to take action in the twenty-first century than for them to cry and lament their condition while asking why we didn't do better when we had the chance. I will educate my children and grandchildren about all things human. Most importantly, I will not decide for them what their futures will be. In fact, I will do everything I can think of to support them as they discover their own natural talents. Might your child be the one who helps planet Earth survive the next catastrophe? Is your child destined to become a giant?

MAY THE FORCE BE WITH US!

Young Artist Discovers a Natural Talent: Photo by Author

Reader's Guide

This book is perfect for group discussion because of the serious nature of its contents. It is especially important to give and receive thoughtful advice, if for no other reason than to better understand some of the subject matter that you or others may not be familiar with. At all times, however, it is up to you to decide what to believe and what to dismiss. Please remember that it is perfectly OK to disagree with others without getting angry. That is the last thing I would want to see happen. Simply agree to disagree if you cannot find common ground on a point of contention, but please don't let that sway you from your path to knowledge.

As you read this book you will quickly understand that this work is just a starting point that can lead you on an adventure of learning, either individually or in a group. It is my hope that many people will take this journey and come to a better understanding of all of these topics and share that knowledge with their families and friends. So, get a group organized, meet up on a slow night for a few hours, and enjoy some face-to-face interaction with other human beings.

You never know, perhaps one of you will even change the world!

ACKNOWLEDGMENTS/DISCLOSURES

This work would not have been possible without the patience and understanding of my friend and life companion, Tanya.

All of the photos used in this work were obtained under license from Dreamstime.com unless otherwise noted.

Illustrations in picture #7 and picture #10 were created by the author.

This is a dated publication. Since new information is becoming available on a continual basis, some information herein may no longer apply. As much as practicable, at the time of publication, I have ensured that the information is up to date.

This work is the result of nearly seventy years of exposure to, and the casual study of various religious teachings and document translations as determined by professionals in various fields of study. I have personally approached all materials used in my research with a critical view to ensure that I correctly understood everything presented and also to ensure the legitimacy of the information presented.

This work is not designed to discourage or offend anyone at any time, either now or in the future. I fully understand the relationship between religion and faith; therefore, have faith in yourself and your own ability to rule your own life. Allow others to do the same. It is my hope that all who read this work will be encouraged to expand their horizons and improve their lives and the lives of their children.

ORIGINAL QUOTES
FROM THIS WORK

"All of the human population on planet Earth is of one family, no matter what our physical appearances say and no matter what any bigot tells you!"

"All knowledge is sacred!"

"Maybe it's true, time heals all things. Maybe, just maybe, time also erases all things."

"Only you can prevent ignorance in your life."

"There is always another secret hiding just beyond the horizon of our present knowledge."

"Perhaps we all should just stop throwing stones."

DEDICATION

This work is dedicated to all the poor souls who have been bamboozled and brainwashed by figures of authority in their lives.

I hereby demand that all parents, teachers, religious leaders, and politicians immediately cease and desist with the propagation and dissemination of false and unfounded lies and deceit that they are heaping on our young children day in and day out to ensure that their fates in life will be as followers instead of the leaders of tomorrow we so dearly need.

Printed in the United States
by Baker & Taylor Publisher Services